Navigation, Strategy and Tactics

Navigation, Strategy and Tactics

Stuart Quarrie

Guardian Newspapers Ltd

Guardian Newspapers Ltd
119 Farringdon Road
London EC1R 3ER

ISBN 0 85265 031 0

Printed and bound in Italy
by Amadeus S.p.A – Rome

Contents

This book is written for sailors of all kinds who want to improve their navigation or tactical skills. In general it is not intended for the complete newcomer to navigation but is written in such a way that even someone with little or no formal navigation training or experience should find it to be of real use. I have tried to write it in such a way that the reader will feel that he or she is almost talking to me while reading. The intention is to take a subject which is still treated like a black art by some and transform it into an easily understood part of sailing.

Almost anyone with an interest in navigation, tactics, electronics or strategy may find the book to be of use; it is specifically intended for readers listed below:

The offshore navigator

Since much of my time is spent navigating yachts around the British coastline, it should not be surprising to find that currents and tides are dealt with in some detail. The sections on planning, strategy and basic techniques will be of particular use offshore - either for racing or for the performance-oriented cruising sailor.

The inshore navigator

Racing around the cans is also covered in depth. Techniques and tips for race navigation in the frenetic conditions experienced inshore are dealt with and of course, much of the strategy is equally valid inshore as well as offshore.

The tactician

On many yachts, especially the smaller ones, the navigator is also the tactician. Even if the jobs are split between two separate people it is vital that the navigator understands the tactical decisions and vice versa. Hence there is a comprehensive chapter on boat-to-boat tactics which covers most situations which can be envisaged in ordinary fleet racing.

The crew

Although aimed at the specialists at the back of the boat, it is important that all members of the crew of a racing yacht have at least some understanding of the roles of the decision makers - if nothing else they can then appreciate the difficulties better, or be able to have a useful input to the decision-making process. This book has been written in such a way that it is readable by all the crew whatever their own specialization.

Race officers

While not a handbook for race officers, the sections dealing with starting, tidal wind and finishing may be of special interest to those good people who spend their weekends making it possible for the rest of us to go racing!

How to use this book

As will already be apparent, this book is laid out more in the style of a good computer manual than most navigation books and this is deliberate. It is not intended that a reader would normally read the book from cover to cover but rather that a particular section or chapter may be read in detail when needed. To this end the book is split into easily identifiable chapters, sections and subsections, each of which is accessible without having to wade through large chunks of unwanted text.

Because the subject is technical, some text would be hard to follow without adequate visual material. This is provided throughout by simple line drawings and diagrams, also numbered and indexed for easy reference.

11 t
set
deg
ang

1   The Team

To achieve good results, I believe that the navigator has to f
with the rest of the crew as part of a cohesive team . . . who
the navigator may be!

If the crew is going to function properly as a team, there n
be mutual trust and, even more important, an understanding of
strengths and weaknesses of each member of the group.
means that it is vital for the whole crew, or at least all of the
members, to sail together often to build up the knowledge requ
to be able to work together efficiently. It is very difficult fe
navigator, however experienced he or she may be, to step on
yacht and give the right information as it is needed.

In my role as navigator I have sailed on hundreds of ya
with almost an equal number of skippers. In my experience e
skipper and tactician will require a slightly different input f
the navigator.

During 1985 I was sailing on an Admiral's Cup triallist ca
Marionette with Jo Richards as skipper. Over the season we
used to each other so that I knew which bits of data he wa
and we worked well together. During the next winter I sailec
the One-Tonner *Jade* in the SORC series and for this I ha
time to prepare; I flew to Florida and the next day we sta
racing. During the first race I gave David Howlett, who
skippering her, the same information that I knew Jo would I
wanted only to find that a lot of this was unnecessary due
David's own skills, whereas I was not giving him other data w
he felt was essential. Needless to say, we did not do as wel
we might have done in the first race . . . but we quickly le
how to sail together and by the second start we were communica
well and went on to win the series.

1.1 MANAGEMENT STRUCTURE

One of the common failings on a lot of cruiser/racers and e
some supposedly flat-out racing campaigns is that there is
proper decision-making and management structure on the ya
In my opinion, although input from anyone on the yacht who
something useful to say is good, the eventual decisions canno
made 'by committee'. This does not mean that all decision
any kind need to be made by the same person, far from it, be

does mean that each decision needs to have one person responsible and accountable for its execution.

On small yachts this will tend to be straightforward since there are less people and therefore the jobs and thus the decision making will be more concentrated. On a larger yacht, though, it can be really critical that the right people are making decisions in their own areas of competence.

Trimmers should (by and large) decide on sail combinations, although this will need to be in consultation with the helmsman when control questions start to come into the reckoning. The helmsman should decide when the yacht feels under- or over-powered and communicate this to the trimmers who then make the decision on correct sail choice. This can occasionally lead to differences of opinion which need to be resolved by 'a higher authority'.

The tactician should decide when and how to sail in relation to other yachts, but the navigator should decide on the optimum overall strategy. Assuming that the navigator and tactician are different people on the yacht, this can obviously lead to complications when the tactics and strategy are in opposition to each other.

Although the tactician will be deciding how the yacht is going to deal with other yachts in the approach to and departure from a mark, the bowman or crew boss will be deciding on the type of drop or hoist to be carried out in the light of the conditions and the navigator will be calculating the optimum courses and sails for the next leg.

There will, therefore, nearly always need to be some form of interaction between differing disciplines on the yacht in order to arrive at almost any decision and in each case one person must have the ultimate authority to make the final decision. The detail of who is responsible for what will obviously differ from yacht to yacht and will be dependent on the relative skills and experience of the various crew members.

In every yacht there must be a final, overall arbiter - the skipper. In the rare cases when the various parties are unable to agree or when there is real doubt as to the best course, the skipper must be prepared to make a decision based on the facts as he sees them. I have found in my sailing and coaching that in a lot of yachts the skipper attempts to make every decision regardless of its nature, and this is probably just as bad as not having anyone making decisions.

In nearly every case it is not good to have the principal helmsman as the main minute-by-minute decision maker. It is unrealistic to expect that enough concentration can be applied to the job of helming as well as to considering other matters, so the helmsman should, wherever possible, be just that. This is where a lot of management problems originate: the helmsman, feeling that he is the only experienced person on the yacht is reluctant to delegate other areas of responsibility to less experienced crew members and thus tries to do everything, with the inevitable result that everything is done badly and the yacht goes slowly in the wrong direction.

Traditional navigator

**1.2
THE ROLE
OF THE
NAVIGATOR**

Traditionally the main task of both cruising and racing navigators was the safe navigation of the yacht, which primarily meant fixing her position and comparing this with known dangers.

When I first started race navigation in the early 1970s this was still the case, most of my time was spent either fixing positions or working out the position by dead reckoning and working up estimated positions. The optimum course to steer was obviously also needed, but since the knowledge of the yacht's position was often only accurate to within one or two miles at the end of an offshore leg of a race, this meant that courses were also approximate.

It used to be important to ensure that your landfall was on the best side of the mark to allow for errors in your fixing; and keeping an up-to-date, detailed log was an art in itself. As a general rule, this form of simple but basic navigation left little time for other tasks; I remember being totally involved in keeping track of where we were, especially when tacking or gybing in bad visibility. At the time, and with the equipment then available, this was the only sensible course of action and many races have been won (and lost) by accurate 'basic' navigation. For better or worse this situation has now largely changed.

The navigator with modern electronics

Nowadays nearly all offshore yachts have one electronic means or another for position fixing. Some of these, like GPS, are accurate nearly all the time, while others, like Decca or Loran, do have their fixed and variable errors to cope with, but most give virtually continuous data on the position of the yacht.

One could be mistaken for thinking that there is no longer a place for a navigator on a racing yacht, but this is far from the truth. For one thing, electronics, however reliable they are, have a habit of ceasing to function at the most inconvenient times and then the navigator needs to be able to revert instantly to more traditional methods. At other times the electronics may give erroneous readings and it is only by keeping an approximate check of the yacht's position by other means that these errors can be picked up.

A lot of other facets of the navigator's job still remain inherently unchanged, from tidal height calculations through to simple (but essential) pilotage in inshore situations. Never be misled into believing too implicitly in the electronics, especially when the difference of a few metres can mean the difference between winning or hitting the bottom.

The biggest change as far as I have been concerned is the freedom which the electronics have given me as a navigator to have an input in other aspects of the performance of the yacht, things for which there simply was not time in the past. The most significant of all these extra tasks has been that of performance monitoring and thus enhancing the ability to give real information on optimum courses to steer. Add to this the fact that the position of the yacht is normally known to within a few tens of metres, even after a long offshore beat in thick fog, and it becomes plain that it is possible to impart really accurate information on courses to steer.

This means that while it is still perfectly feasible to revert to 'old-fashioned' techniques, and indeed it is sometimes vital to do so, it is not possible to have the same kind of accuracy without the modern electronics. Thus the yacht without an electronic position fixer is at a real disadvantage. This can be taken too far, however: I have heard of at least one yacht retiring from a race simply because her Decca had gone down!

Increasingly it is important to have as navigator someone who is familiar with the internal workings of the electronic boxes as well as their associated wiring, and who can keep them going in adverse conditions. The navigator's role has changed with the increasing use of silicon chips, but it is still as vital as ever and in my experience is still just as much fun as it ever was.

5 Sha
cours

Basic Navigation Techniques

This book is not aimed at the newcomer to navigation and the reader may well be wondering why it includes this chapter entitled 'basic navigation techniques'. The reason is that over the past several years, I have found that no two navigators operate in quite the same way and most have some techniques and shortcuts which they use to make their own lives easier. This chapter is here to ensure that we are all speaking the same language through the rest of the book and to pass on some of the basic ideas which I have developed in my own sailing and racing.

There are four different sources of tidal stream data which need to be taken into account while racing in tidal waters.

Tidal diamonds

On British Admiralty charts the tidal stream information is presented in a tabular format for various selected points on the chart. The information is always given hour by hour with timing based on the high-water times for a suitable 'standard port'. Two figures for the rate are given, a mean spring and a mean neap rate, and directions are given in degrees true towards which the tide is flowing, an example of such a table is shown in diagram 1.

Streams referred to HW at Plymouth (Devonport)

⟨A⟩	50°09' .5N 4°34' .7W		⟨B⟩	50°12' .4N 4°23' .8W	
339	0.2	0.1	358	0.6	0.3
005	0.6	0.3	011	0.9	0.4
022	0.9	0.4	016	1.6	0.8
023	0.6	0.3	024	1.2	0.7
022	0.4	0.2	033	0.7	0.4
036	0.2	0.1	034	0.1	0.0
	0.0	0.0	178	0.4	0.2
217	0.3	0.1	196	1.1	0.6
213	0.5	0.2	196	2.2	1.2
207	0.7	0.3	198	2.6	1.4
190	0.8	0.4	189	1.8	0.9
180	0.5	0.2	203	0.7	0.3
276	0.1	0.0	324	0.3	0.1

ole
iralty

There are two areas of possible confusion which I have found to exist in the use of such a table, the first being how to use the times. If we took a day when high water Plymouth was at, say, 1210, then the hour in the table called 'HW' would actually relate to the time from 1140 until 1240; that is it would be the hour centred around high water. 'HW - 1' would refer to 1040 until 1140, and so on. It is important to remember that the rates and directions given are averages for the whole hour and near the turn of the tide may need to be looked at in conjunction with the hours before or after in order to get a realistic picture of what is happening.

The second possible area of confusion lies in the terms 'mean spring' and 'mean neap'. The rates are given for a tide which has an average range (difference between high and low water heights) for either spring or neap tides. These average ranges can be found from the tide tables and are normally given in the form of a little table within the tidal curve for the standard port. Since these averages do not necessarily relate in any way to the current ranges at the top of springs or the bottom of neaps, you must always go back to the actual range for 'today' and compare this with the mean ranges, rather than thinking whether it is neaps or springs on that day.

To look at an example based on Portsmouth, where the mean spring range is 4.1m and the mean neap range is 2.0m, might make this distinction clearer. In one particular fortnight during 1991 the highest range at springs was 4.5m and the lowest range during the same fortnight was 1.6m. If you were considering a tide a few days before the top of springs, then the range may have been 4.1m. Compared to the mean ranges this is obviously an average spring tide, while within the particular fortnight it is nowhere near the highest tide. If during the same fortnight you were looking at the streams at the top of springs, it would be necessary to extrapolate beyond the normal spring rate quite considerably.

The final area of possible error when using information from tidal diamonds is in interpolation between adjacent diamonds. Here you need to use common sense and look at the underwater topography to decide which diamonds most nearly apply to your position and how they relate to each other.

Interpolation between springs and neaps

Having just seen the importance of comparing the real tidal ranges with mean values for springs and neaps it is worth looking at the actual process of comparison.

Since the rates of tidal stream are given for two mean ranges of tide (spring and neap), it is possible to plot these positions on a graph and consider that all other rates relate in the same way; that is, that the graph joining our two points is a straight line. It would then be possible to compare any other range algebraically to get the rate of tide for 'today'.

Thus, if still using Portsmouth as the example with mean ranges of 4.1m and 2.0m at springs and neaps, if the range today were 3.5m and if the rates of tide given by the Admiralty were, say, 2.8m at springs and 1.4m at neaps, then it is possible to work out the rate at present as follows:

INTERPOLATION - METHOD 1

RATE NOW = (range x 2)/(mean spring range + mean neap
range) x (spring rate + neap rate)/2
= (3.5 x 2)/ (4.1 + 2.0) x (2.8 + 1.4)/2
= 2.4 knots

Now, while this sort of sum is possible for those with a mathematical bent, it is not very feasible for most of us, especially since it may be necessary to perform a lot of such calculations even in a short race.

It is possible to simplify the above equation slightly by making the assumption that the straight line between springs and neaps goes to zero rate at zero range. This enables one to compare today's range with just the spring range and the spring rate in order to work out today's rate. Thus using the same example as before:

INTERPOLATION - METHOD 2

RATE NOW = range/spring range x spring rate
= 3.5 / 4.1 x 2.8
= 2.39 knots

However, I find that even this relatively easy calculation becomes tedious in a real racing situation and prefer to use an approximation which is pretty accurate and which can be worked out in my head whenever needed.

For this, I calculate a factor to relate the range for today with the mean ranges at springs and neaps, and then apply this 'springiness' factor to any rate which is required. Once again, using the same example as before:

INTERPOLATION - METHOD 3 - PREFERRED

FACTOR = (spring range - range today) / (spring range - neap
range)
= (4.1 - 3.5) / (4.1 - 2.0)
= 0.6 / 2.1
= approximately $1/3$

Applying this factor, in this case to a spring rate of 2.8m and neap of 1.4m works as follows:

$$\text{RATE} = \text{spring rate} - ((\text{spring rate} - \text{neap rate}) \times \text{factor})$$
$$= 2.8 - ((\ 2.8 - 1.4 \ ) \times {}^1\!/_3)$$
$$= 2.8 - (1.4 \ / \ 3)$$
$$= 2.8 - 0.5$$
$$= 2.3 \text{ knots}$$

At first sight this may look even more complicated th
calculations done before, but the magic lies in the fact t
factor only needs to be calculated once for each day a
simple fraction can then be applied to any rates at will. It
even when jumping between standard ports and can b
equally well with tidal diamond information or that gi
Admiralty tidal stream atlases.

Admiralty tidal stream atlases

Tidal stream atlases (whoever produces them) are me
pictorial way of presenting the information which is avail
tabular form on Admiralty charts. For the yachtsman,
particular for the racing sailor, they have some major adva
when compared to tidal diamond tables. The chief among
advantages being that someone has spent a lot of time and
interpolating between the points on the chart for whic
information is available in order to be able to present a 'p
of the streams for an area. This will invariably be more ac
than any attempt to interpolate between adjacent diamon
could be made on the yacht, especially while racing.

The other real bonus for most navigators is that a pic
easier to interpret than a table (except for a few pe
mathematicians among our ranks).

It must be remembered that the timings for each page
one hour before HW, etc.) work in the same way as they
tidal diamond information and that it is equally import
interpolate between the figures given for spring rates and
rates as it was before. For those navigators who are not u
sailing in UK waters it is also worth pointing out that the
for the figures given on an Admiralty atlas is, for example, '2
but this means 2.8 knots at mean spring range and 1.4 kr
mean neap range and not, as one student of mine once th
28.14 knots! Incidentally, the point between the numbers
the exact spot at which the data was measured.

Reeves-Fowkes tidal atlases

It is not just the Admiralty who publish tidal atlases, the
several privately produced booklets some of which provide ex
additional information.

One area particularly well covered is the English Chann
which there is a range of atlases compiled by Michael R

Fowkes. These are quite different from the Admiralty atlases
several ways. They are all based on Cherbourg as their stand
port and give one average figure for the tidal stream rate at e
point. There is then a look-up table to relate these average ra
to the actual height of high water on the day in question wh
means that there is never any need for interpolation.

These atlases also contain another look-up table for ti
heights at various ports and harbours around the coast, obviat
the need to calculate tidal heights. Anyone who is seriously rac
in the English Channel should at least consider getting copies
the relevant atlases in this series.

Home-made atlases

I find that extracting tidal stream information from the tidal diamo
on charts is a long-winded process, especially if you are hav
to use several charts in order to obtain the necessary informati
Therefore, if I am going to race in a tidal area for which there
not a commercially available tidal stream atlas I like to spe
some time beforehand preparing my own; I draw a sketch map
the area and then laboriously extract the information from
tables on the charts and interpolate between diamonds wh
necessary until I have a local atlas of my own. This is invaria
better than trying to do the same thing while actually racing wh
there is never enough time to consider all the available informat
properly.

Measured tidal streams

One of the checks which I have always carried out on longer rac
even before the advent of good electronic fixing aids, is
compare my estimate of tidal drift with what is actually happen
by comparing fixes with estimated positions. This was o
possible over fairly long periods of time (say longer than 15 minu
and was only useful as a long-term check that the right sort
data was being used.

With the advent of GPS as a fixing system, it has beco
possible to compare accurately one's course and speed over
ground with course and speed through the water on a realistica
short time scale. This means that it is now feasible to get a read
from the instruments of tidal stream rate and direction and m
good racing systems will allow this as a standard option (
chapters 7 and 8 for more detail). This provides enormous n
potential for monitoring the rate and direction of the stream on
ongoing basis and enables changes over as short a time as
seconds to be noted. This is really useful for seeing when you
in (or out) of areas of strong stream and also for seeing exac
when the tide is turning.

Those unfortunates who are still stuck with Decca or Loran

the fixing system will find that, although the same comparisons between ground and water track are possible, the errors in the systems mean that it is important to have been on a steady course and speed for about five minutes in order to get a good readout of current; this virtually precludes the use of the facility for short-term tidal stream analysis.

Extracting several hours of tide from an atlas

When racing on a leg which is going to take several hours in a tidal situation, it is not always easy to extract the rates and direction for each hour, partly at least because you need to know where you will be during each hour and even quite small differences in boat speed can add up to large positional changes.

I use the simple method of having some card (plain post cards are ideal) marked up along their edges with various boat speeds to the scale of the tidal atlas. For a 40ft yacht I would normally have cards marked for speeds from, say, four knots up to 10 knots at half-knot intervals. Once close to the next mark so that an approximate rounding time is known, I then flip through the tidal atlas with the most likely speed cards marking them with the rate and direction of the stream for each hour.

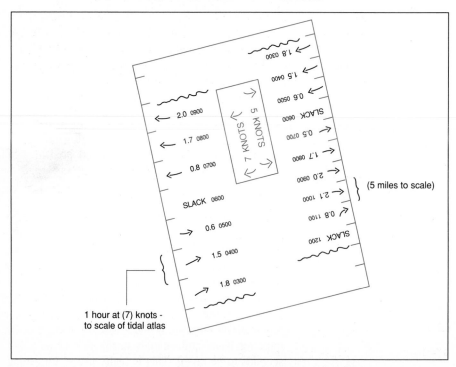

2 Card for tidal stream extraction

Because the cards are made to scale, your approximate position is easily determined just by placing the card so that it is aligned correctly with the atlas and always has the same point against the first and last marks. If it is considered that the yacht will be off track due to strong cross tide then an appropriate allowance does need to be made, but at least the card edge gives a good starting position.

At least one navigator I know has taken this idea one stage further and has had made some thin transparent plastic strips with the speed scales permanently marked so that the idea can be used more readily on the side deck.

2.2 TIDAL HEIGHTS

Tidal heights need to be worked out so that you know when it is safe to go over potentially dangerous areas and also so that an estimate can be made of how close it is possible to sail to a shoreline. In some situations it is also useful to know how far a particular danger will be exposed to make identification simpler.

In most sailing areas it is sufficient to use the nearest standard port, correct for secondary port differences and then use the 'twelfth's rule' to calculate the actual heights for any given time. For those who are not familiar with the twelfth's rule, it uses the fact that for most areas the tide rises and falls in a way which approximates to a sine curve and that in the first and last hours of rise (or fall) the tide will change by $1/12$ of the range, in the second and fifth hours it will change by $2/12$, while in the third and fourth hours it will be altering at its maximum and will change by $3/12$ of the range. Strictly speaking one should refer to sixths of the duration rather than to hours either side of high water but in most cases this can be largely ignored, bearing in mind the other inaccuracies with the twelfth's rule (see diagrams 3 – 4).

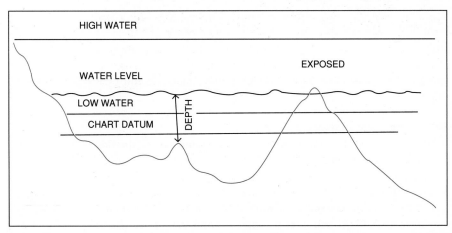

HIGH WATER

WATER LEVEL

EXPOSED

LOW WATER

DEPTH

CHART DATUM

3 Tidal levels

There are some areas for which the twelfth's rule gives errors which are unacceptably large due to unevenly shaped tidal curves. In such areas it is better to use the actual tidal curve for the nearest standard port to calculate from unless only a very approximate height is required.

2

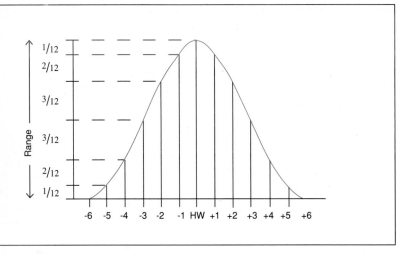

elfths rule'

Once again, sailors in the English Channel are very fortunate in having the Michael Reeves-Fowkes tidal atlases since these give look-up tables for each hour of tidal height at most places around the coast.

As a general principle, I like to work out tidal heights as accurately as possible, normally to within 0.1m, and then apply my own safety margins, rather than being less accurate initially. This ensures that I understand and fully appreciate the level of risk at any given time. The amount of safety margin will obviously depend on the type of sea bed and on the conditions at the time in question.

2.1
TID
STR

ING A
RSE TO
ER

There are basically two different types of course shaping. There is the fairly accurate short-term shaping, where one is only dealing with at most a couple of hours; then there is the less accurate type of shaping where a long cross-tide leg is being sailed which is going to take several hours and possibly more than one full tidal sequence.

1 Ti
from
cha

Short-term course shaping

In this case it is important to get the direction and rate of the tide correct as well as estimating the boat speed as accurately as possible. Having done these two things, a simple triangle is then the easiest way to sort out the best course to steer.

If the conditions are such that some leeway is likely, this should be added into the correction as an angular adjustment *towards* the wind after the triangle has been resolved. Most modern cruiser/racers make negligible leeway in average conditions but can make considerable leeway in both very light and very rough conditions. You must get used to the yacht on which you sail in order to get a feel for the numbers involved, but typically leeway angles of say two-three degrees might be used in moderate conditions, rising to 10° in light airs when the boat speed is well below hull speed and possibly up to 15° in really steep seas, especially if the wind has dropped somewhat while leaving the waves.

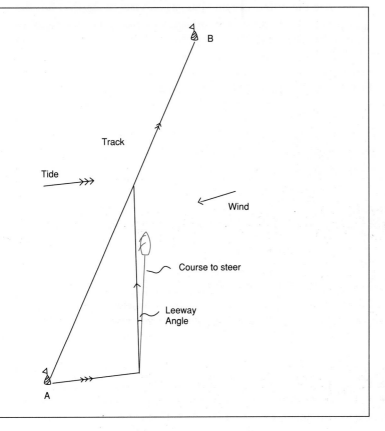

Notes:

1. All the tide should be put on at the beginning in one-hour blocks.

2. The same number of hours (or proportion of an hour) must be used for the line of boat speed as was used for the tide.

3. It is nearly always simplest to work in a convenient scale (say 4cm = 1 mile) rather than trying to utilize the scale of the chart - as long as all sides of the triangle are to the same scale all will be well!

4. Add an estimate of leeway *towards* the wind after the tidal triangle has been completed.

Shaping for a long leg

If shaping a course for a leg in excess of about two hours, it is pointless to try to pretend that this will be accurate. In a motor cruiser when the throttle can be set and left it is possible to be accurate, but in a racing yacht, even with the best forecasting in the world, it is unrealistic to expect to be better than 10-15 per cent accurate in your estimate of boat speed over long periods.

The method of course shaping which I apply in these cases is to extract the tidal stream data as described earlier for the approximate time that I think the leg will take, then add up all of the similar tides and cancel opposite ones against each other so that I am left with one aggregate tidal stream vector for the whole leg, even if it is going to take 10 or 12 hours. This vector can then be plotted as a single, simple offset.

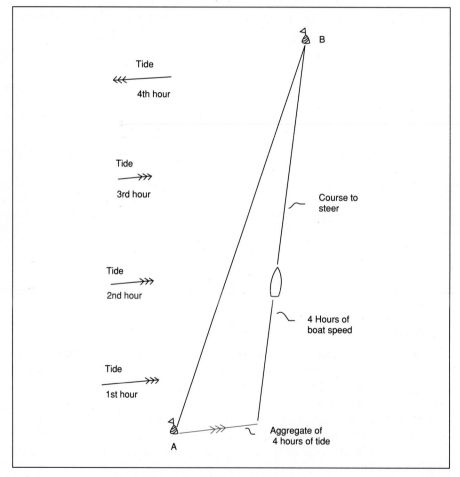

6 Shaping a course - Several hours

One important thing in a case like this is to consider what will happen to the course to steer if the boat speed is either faster or slower than your estimate. I would therefore normally work out the tidal streams for speeds a knot either side of my best guess in order to be able to compare required courses. It is then an easy matter to make adjustments if the speed drops or increases as you are sailing the leg, without having immediately to do a lot of new calculations.

**2.4
THE
1-IN-60
RULE**

There are lots of occasions, chiefly while sitting on the rail in the rain, when it is impractical to draw vector triangles of any kind whether they are for course shaping, new wind on the next leg, or whatever. On these occasions it is handy to have a way of approximating a vector triangle in your head in order to come up with a reasonably accurate answer and the '1-in-60 rule' does just this.

To understand how the rule works it is necessary to look at diagram 7. From this one can see that if looking at a triangle with a 60-mile side to it, one mile offset at the end of 60 miles would give an angle offset of one degree. This is straightforward and merely relies on the way that nautical miles and degrees are linked.

7 '1-in-60 rule'

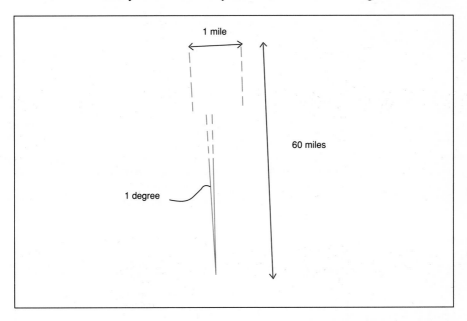

Carrying the process one stage further, it can be seen in the next diagram that over the same 60-mile leg, five miles offset would give a five-degree angle, eight miles an eight-degree angle, and so on.

8 '1-in-60 rule'
- Angles =

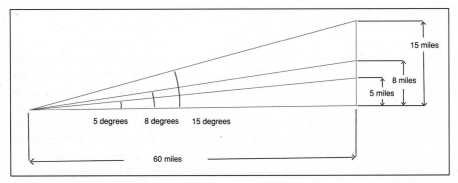

For really accurate shaping of the course to steer, this ͓
is obviously not quite correct. The tide should be laid o͏
start of the leg and the boat speed (or distance run) dra͏
the end of the tidal vector. Now, in addition to the abov͏
can remember back to geometry lessons at school, you wi͏
that if a 'similar' triangle is drawn, it will have the sam͏
and will merely be a different size to the original. Thu͏
take a triangle with a six-mile side as in diagram 9, this is͏
triangle to one with a 60-mile side but one tenth of ͏
Therefore, one tenth of a mile offset will give one degre͏
while one mile will give 10°.

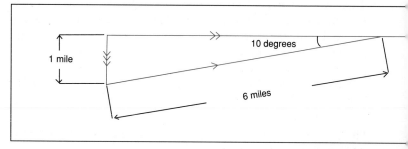

9 '1-in-60 rule' -
Similar triangles

If our boat speed was always six knots, it would ͏
possible to shape courses from this example - a cross tid͏
knot would need 10° offset, a 1.2-knot tide would need 1͏
and a 2.5-knot tide would need a 25° offset as in the next ͏

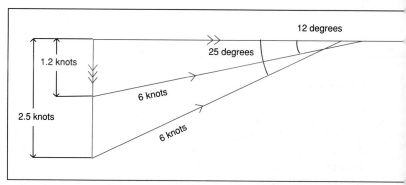

10 '1-in-60 rule'
- at 6 knots,
Angle = 10 x
offset

However, since we do not always want to work at si͏
it is necessary to think of a relationship between the speed͏
of the triangle side) and the offset which will work ͏
number. This comes back to a proportion of 1:60. Since c͏
gives a one degree offset over 60 miles, we can easily w͏
the formula which applies in other cases, thus:

OFFSET in degrees = (60/speed) x offset in miles

So at five knots and with a cross tide of 1.0 knot we wo͏

OFFSET = 60/5 x 1.0
       = 12 x 1.0
       = 12°

and at eight knots' boat speed with a 2.3-knot cross tide the sum would work out as follows:

OFFSET = 60/8 x 2.3
       = 7.5   x 2.3
       = about 17°.

Thus, as long as the long triangle side (speed) is kept to simple numbers, it should be possible to work out any course shaping where the tide is at (or near) right angles to the track. It is equally possible to solve any other right-angled triangle using the same principles. The problem with the above method of approximation is what you should do if the tide (or whatever) is not at right angles.

With the tidal offset being at an angle to the track anywhere up to about 20° to a right angle, the angular offset will be near enough at its maximum.

As the tidal offset comes nearer in line with the track, the offset

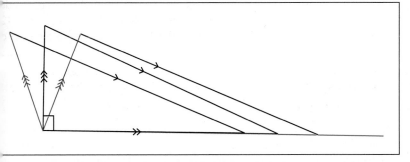

m off-
20
right

will gradually be reduced. By the time the tidal offset is at about 60° (or 120°) to the track, the angular difference will have fallen to approximately 3/4 of the maximum value. With a tidal angle of 45°, the offset will be 2/3 and when the tidal angle is 30° the offset will have fallen to 1/2 of the maximum (see diagram 12).

Below this the angle offset for normal rates of tide produce such small angle offsets as to be fairly insignificant and if required it is better either to draw the triangle or do a trigonometric calculation in order to obtain an accurate answer.

The other time that this system of approximation does not work is when the ratio of tide to boat speed would give angle offsets in excess of 30°. Here the geometry really starts to fall apart and it is once again better to revert to basics. With a tide at right angles this will not happen until the tide is half the boat speed,

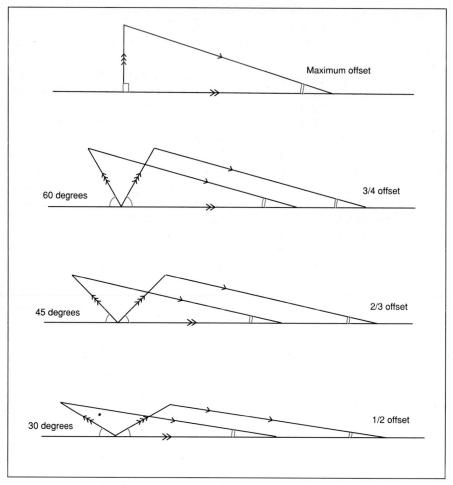

Maximum offset

60 degrees

3/4 offset

45 degrees

2/3 offset

30 degrees

1/2 offset

12 Offset
compared
to tidal angle

when it is so important to get it right that doing a drawing should not seem too unreasonable.

Obviously this approximation method can be used in any triangle and is useful not only for shaping courses but also for seeing how much the wind will change when the tide turns, working out laylines in a cross tide, calculating the new wind on the next leg of the course and so on.

2.5 WIND–DRIVEN CURRENTS

For those of us who are most used to sailing in areas with strong tidal streams, the idea of powerful currents which are generated just by the wind will seem somewhat unlikely. In the tidal situation the water flow changes direction completely every six hours or so and this largely prevents wind-driven currents from being set up, although they can of course alter the rate of the tidal stream and possibly the time that the tide turns. In areas where the tidal flow is either weak or non existent, however, it is possible and even quite normal to get fairly strong currents generated as a result of a wind blowing consistently from one direction.

In the open ocean it is thought that after several hours with a steady wind it is usual to get a wind-generated current of up to 1/50th of the wind speed. Thus a wind of force six (about 25 knots) would give 1/2 knot of current, while a full gale blowing at 50 knots would give a current of one knot. These figures are for the open ocean and in the more confined water in which most of us sail it is possible to get local wind-driven currents which exceed these rates quite considerably.

If, for example, there is a 1/2-knot current flowing and this then meets a headland or other constriction, then the rate of the current may double or even triple in a very short distance. The same principle will apply to local areas of shallow water. In some passages between islands in the Baltic or Mediterranean it is quite common to get wind-driven currents of up to three or four knots on a day with a steady force four.

Even a sea breeze lasting perhaps eight hours can be enough

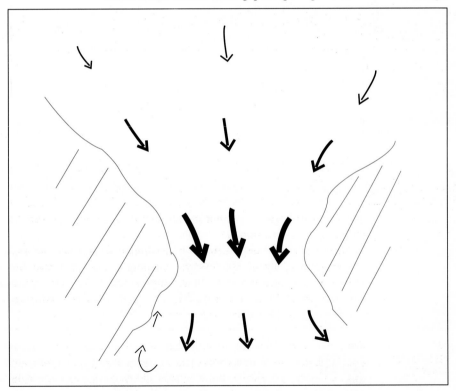

13 Current Increases if flow constricted

to generate quite strong currents, a phenomenon which I experienced recently in Sicily while sailing from the harbour of Palermo. Here the sea breeze develops a gentle current into the bay of Palermo of perhaps 1/2 knot; obviously all the water going into the bay has to come out again somewhere and it does this

as a current of about 1.5 knots running along the coas
to sea around the nearby headland.

It is normally possible to use common sense to 'gue

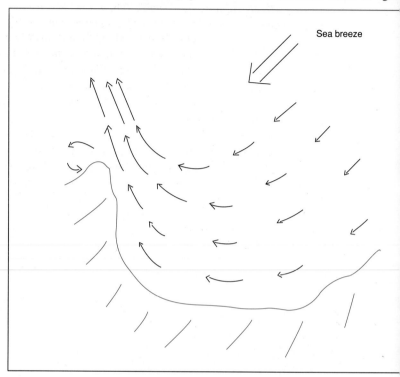

Sea breeze

14 Bay of
Palermo - wind-
driven current

the effect of a particular wind direction on the sea surfac
judge where the strongest and weakest wind-driven cur
likely to be. Any constriction to the water flow, especial
end of a long open expanse of water is going to give an
in the current rate. Conversely, sheltered areas of wate
behind an island or headland, should give relief from th
and in some cases you may even experience counter cur
up as swirls. In the absence of more detailed, local infc
the Admiralty Pilot books are usually helpful in area
experience consistent wind-driven currents.

**2.6
PLOTTING
LATITUDE
AND
LONGITUDE**

There are times when it is necessary to plot a position in
and longitude even in these days of electronic wizardry
worth having a simple and quick system for such plotting
leaving the subject of electronic wizardry, it must be said
silicon chip offers the quickest and simplest methods c
particular with the 'Yeoman Plotter' which is described i
more detail in chapter 8.

In principle it is simple to plot a position using latit
longitude on a chart - simply transfer the position from

and top (or bottom) of the chart and where the two points m
is your position. In practice, however, there are easy ways of do
this and difficult ways.

Probably one of the most difficult ways, especially while sitt
with the chart on your knee while on the side deck, is to ge
pair of parallel rulers and draw lines from the relevant points
the chart edge to where the two lines join. This does work on
chart table but it is unnecessarily difficult and is often inaccura
I only mention it because it is a method taught at a great m:
navigation theory classes (in the main I suspect by ex-big s
navigators).

The method which I prefer is to use a pair of dividers
measure the distance from a convenient line on the chart to
latitude and transfer this to the approximate longitude before putt
a pencil mark on the chart. Next I do the same with the longitu
but this time I already have the latitude marked fairly close to
correct place. It is then simple to marry the two marks up visu.
with no further measuring being necessary.

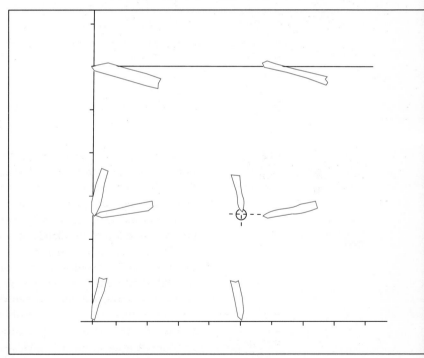

15 Plotting
latitude and
longitude

Another thing which really makes life easy is to have
latitude and longitude scales marked on the chart indelibly al
most grid lines. This enables you to see both latitude :
longitude, no matter how the chart is folded.

In some cases it may also be worth drawing more grid li
perhaps at three- or four-centimetre intervals to give a really e

visual reference. On some charts this might cause confusion, so care is needed before adding too much.

2.7 TRUE OR MAGNETIC

One of my pet hates is the dogmatic navigator who states categorically that one should *always* plot in degrees true (or magnetic depending on his background). In fact, of course, with the right sort of plotting instrument it is equally accurate to plot using either degrees true or degrees magnetic and it cannot really matter which system is used - as long as you, the navigator, do not get confused.

I usually utilize a Breton Plotter for most chart work and since this has its own compass rose built in, it is just as easy to plot using either true or magnetic. In my own navigation, I therefore plot in magnetic if the number I am dealing with is derived from a magnetic source (eg. compass bearing) or if it is going to be used with a magnetic compass (eg. course to steer). When a number is given in degrees true (eg. tidal stream from a tidal diamond, or transit on an Admiralty chart), then I will plot it in degrees true.

I like to have all electronic sources of bearings, such as Decca or GPS, giving their bearings in degrees magnetic so that I know that their output can be transferred straight to compass courses without needing correction for variation.

Thus, I nearly always use degrees magnetic because I find it more convenient to do so, but on any occasion when it is simpler to use degrees true then once again I am quite happy. This way I rarely need to do a conversion from degrees true to magnetic, or vice versa, and can never make an arithmetic mistake. I should add that the system only works if your compasses are well-corrected so that there is no deviation to apply.

2.8 CLEARING LINES

In both racing and cruising pilotage I have found the use of clearing lines to be one of the most useful and least-used methods of navigation.

The principle is very simple: if you have a danger which you must keep clear of and have a clearing line as in diagram 16, then you do not need to know where you are but simply that you are the safe side of the line. If the line can be derived from something which is visually easy to spot, such as a good transit, then you hardly need to work at all in order to stay safe, just keep half an eye on the transit to make sure that you are not straying into danger (see diagram 16).

Even when it is not possible to find a convenient transit, a bearing taken on a prominent object is not at all difficult to keep track of, but here it is important to be aware of how close the clearing line passes to the danger and also with what degree of accuracy you are able to take the bearing.

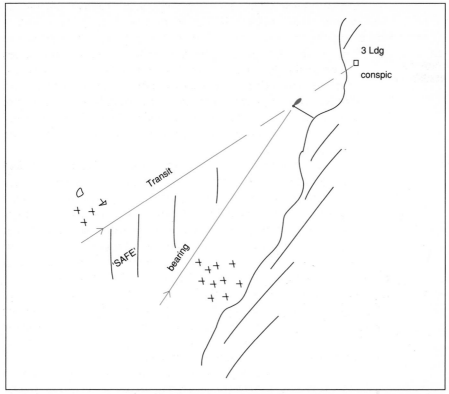

3 Ldg

conspic

Transit

'SAFE'

bearing

16 Clearing lines   It is not difficult to use an electronic fixer to give you a clearing line and the mechanics of this are described in chapter 8.

2.9 TIDAL LAYLINES

Sailing in current or a tidal stream there will inevitably come a time when you want to find the tacking or gybing layline to a mark in a cross tide. The first time that I tried to solve this problem I spent ages working out how to do it and felt that a simple explanation here would be worthwhile.

In essence the problem is the same as shaping a course to steer, except that in this case you have no option as to your course (decided by the wind direction and your optimum course upwind) but you do have choice as to your starting position - that is, when you put in your final tack.

When sailing up a beat you should always make an effort to notice the tacking angle in the particular conditions prevailing at that time and therefore you should know what your course will be on the opposite tack, even without anything more sophisticated than a compass. This means that if there was no tidal stream, the layline would be reached when the buoy was bearing the course on the new tack.

To work out the tidally corrected layline you will of course need to have a good idea of the tidal stream rate and direction,

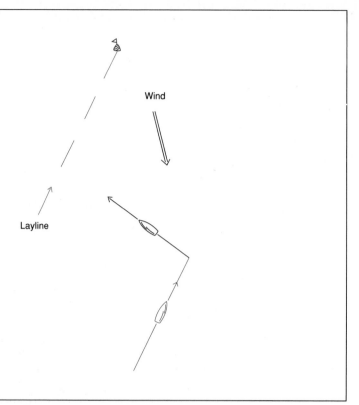

Wind

Layline

ayline -
de

either from the instruments or from basic data sources. It is then a simple matter to draw a triangle as in diagram 18 to calculate the ground track that the yacht will make on the opposite tack.

If the drawing is done using the buoy as the starting point, then it can be seen that this ground track is also the bearing that the buoy should be on for the layline. It will not matter how far away from the buoy you are when the layline is reached as long as the wind does not change direction (see diagram 19).

One additional problem in a beating situation with a lot of cross tide will be that you may well be beating up a shoreline, staying out of the current and having to judge the layline for a buoy which is out in the tide. There are two problems here: the first is that you must guess how strong the tide will be as you leave the shore and, secondly, the wind will change as you sail out into the tide. This latter problem is dealt with fully in the next chapter (tidal wind) and suffice it to say here that the basic problem is still the same.

Another time that judging the layline will not be quite as simple is on a beat when you have not tacked for a considerable time and do not know what the tacking angle will be, at least not from recent data. This is one reason why it is so important to keep good records of the boat's performance so that you do

18 Finding
ground track

know, at least approximately, what angle she will tack through in most conditions and wind strengths.

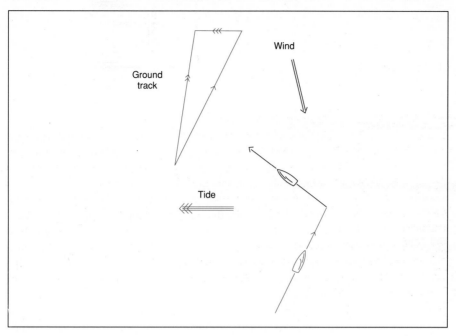

19 Tidal layline

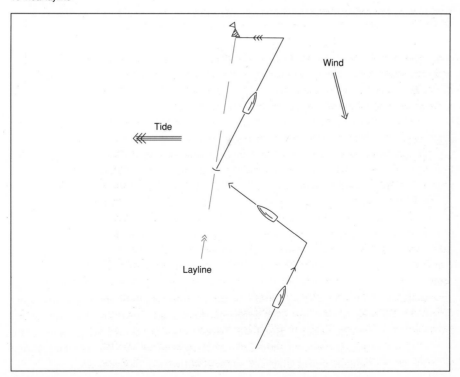

3   Some Race Navigation Concepts

This chapter looks at some of the basic concepts and wind triangles which are needed by the racing navigator. It is particularly aimed at the person who has previously navigated cruising yachts to whom some of the concepts are likely to be new.

3.1 APPARENT AND TRUE WIND

If you stand still on land, the wind you feel is the *true* wind. This is the wind as it really is, unaffected by movement. If you then start moving, let's say running towards the wind, you will immediately experience a different wind caused by a combination of your movement and the true wind - this new wind is called the *apparent* wind.

To apply this analogy to the sailing situation: when the yacht is stationary the masthead instruments measure the true wind, while as soon as the yacht is moving they measure the apparent wind. This is shown in diagram 20.

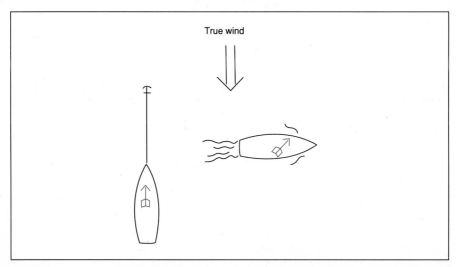

True wind

20 Apparent wind

The apparent wind is thus a combination of two components of wind - the true wind plus the wind caused by the movement of the yacht. Because both components are using the same measurements, they can be thought of as two vectors and drawn together in a diagram such as shown by diagram 21.

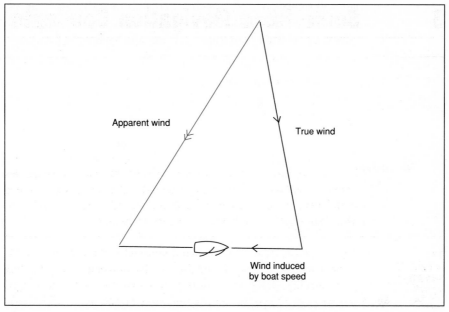

21 Apparent
wind triangle

If you consider what is happening here, the movement of the yacht will always generate a head wind which will move the apparent wind closer to ahead than the true wind. This is true regardless of the point of sailing you happen to be on at the time.

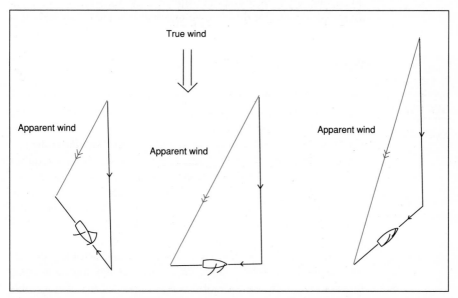

22 Apparent
wind is forward
of true wind

However, the strength of the apparent wind will often also differ from that of the true wind, but this will depend on your point of sailing. In simple terms, if the true wind is forward of the beam then the apparent wind will be stronger than the true wind and vice versa if the true wind is aft of the beam. With the true wind on (or nearly on) the beam, there will be little or no difference in wind speed between true and apparent winds.

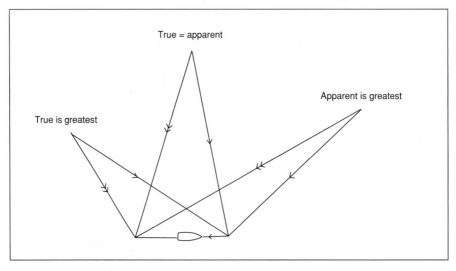

True = apparent

Apparent is greatest

True is greatest

23 True wind speed versus apparent wind speed

Most modern linked instrument systems can give readouts of both true and apparent wind. They do this by taking the raw measurements of apparent wind and boat speed and calculating the combination in much the same way as we have done in the diagrams above. For this to give reasonably accurate answers it is vital that the raw data is as good as possible and calibration of the instruments is normally required. This is covered in some depth in chapter 7.

3.2 NEW WIND ON THE NEXT LEG

One task which the racing navigator has to undertake which is rarely thought of by cruising sailors is establishing what will the wind be on the next leg of the course. In a cruising situation it is nearly always possible to arrive at a corner and decide on the sail combination after the new course has been set. If this requires sailing off course for a few minutes then no harm is done, you just arrive at your destination a little later. On the racing yacht, where places are often won or lost by seconds, it is really important to be able to decide on the right sails for the next leg in plenty of time before you arrive at the mark.

If you are lucky enough to have a sophisticated set of instruments such as the B&G #690 system, these will probably have a *next-leg* function, but in the absence of this it is important that you are able to work out what the new wind will be from first principles. Having said that, in my experience the most accurate way to judge which sails are right for the next leg is to watch the rest of the fleet and copy the best of them! This has the dual disadvantages that it does not work at night and you need to be near the rear of the fleet.

Diagram 24 shows an example of next-leg calculations based on the assumption that the yacht only has very basic instruments with primary readouts - ie. apparent wind speed and angle and boat speed. It can be seen that there are effectively three steps: first work out what the true wind direction and speed is, second calculate the course to steer on the next leg (allowing for tide if appropriate), and finally determine what the new apparent wind will be.

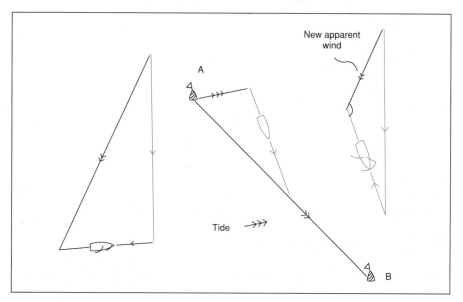

24 New wind on the next leg - basics

The next diagram shows a simplified route to achieve the same ends. The three triangles are amalgamated to reduce the number of lines which are needed and in fact the true wind never needs to be known since it is merely an intermediate step (see diagram 25).

If your instruments give a true wind angle and speed readout then the calculation is even easier, as shown in diagram 26. Here the true wind angle off the bow is related to north in order to orientate it with the chart. It is possible to do this numerically, but in most cases it will prove to be easier to draw in the yacht's heading first and then apply the true wind angle to this. This saves the drawing of one line compared to the more simple instrument system.

If your instruments are also linked to an electronic compass, then one less line still can be drawn.

3.3 TIDAL WIND

So far in this chapter we have talked about *true* and *apparent* winds. However, the term 'true wind' is something of a misnomer. In most situations there will be some current or tidal stream and this will affect the wind in which we sail.

If we start by examining a fairly simple situation, the principle of *tidal wind* should become apparent (excuse the pun!). If

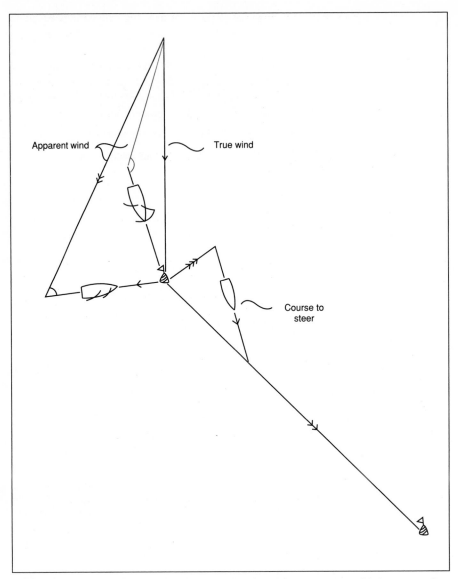

Apparent wind

True wind

Course to steer

25 New wind on the next leg - with apparent wind

anchored on a day when there is a strong tidal stream but absolutely no wind, the instruments and sails will obviously measure zero. However, once the anchor is raised and the yacht starts drifting off down tide, a wind which is equal in strength but opposite in direction to the tide will appear to spring up. This is just like any other wind which is induced by motion and is exemplified in diagram 27.

The next stage is to consider a more realistic sailing day: the same yacht is anchored in the same tidal stream but this time there is some wind even while at anchor. Diagram 28 shows that this time when the anchor is raised and the yacht starts to drift the

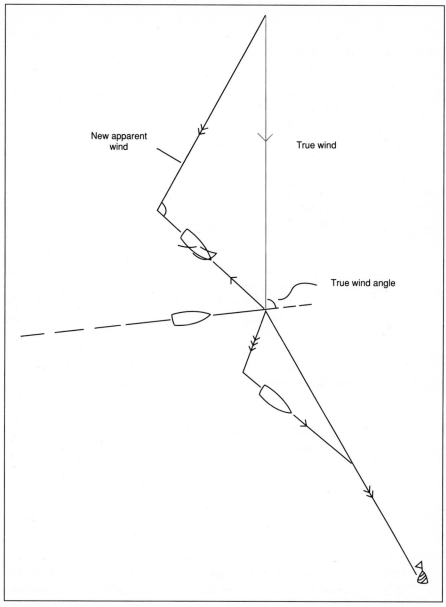

New apparent wind

True wind

True wind angle

26 New wind on the next leg - with magnetic wind direction or true wind angle

wind will be a combination of the *true* wind and the *tidal wind*. These can be added together to give the *true sailing wind* or *sailing wind* for short.

This sailing wind is the wind which all yachts sail in all the time, whether or not they realize that it is not true wind as felt by someone stationary. It does not matter which point of sailing or which tack the yacht is sailing on, it will always experience the same sailing wind until either the underlying true wind or the tidal stream change. Because of the potential for confusion over

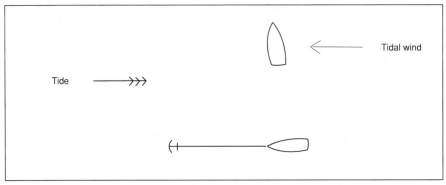

the term 'true wind' I normally use the term *ground wind* to mean the wind without any tidal effect.

If the tidal stream changes then so will the sailing wind. This can be vitally important to the navigator, especially on light-wind days when the proportion of the sailing wind generated by the current is at its largest. Using the 1-in-60 approximations dealt with in the previous chapter, it can be seen that a two-knot stream perpendicular to an eight-knot wind would shift the wind by 15°. Thus if the tide was going at two knots one way and then changed direction and flowed at the same speed in the opposite direction, this would cause a 30° wind shift if the ground wind was eight knots.

On the other hand, if the wind and stream are in line with each other there would be little or no change in direction but a substantial change in wind speed as the tide turned. Using the same figures as above, an eight-knot ground wind would alter into a 10-knot sailing wind with the tide going one way and then die to six knots once the tide had turned - once again a very significant change.

28 Sailing wind

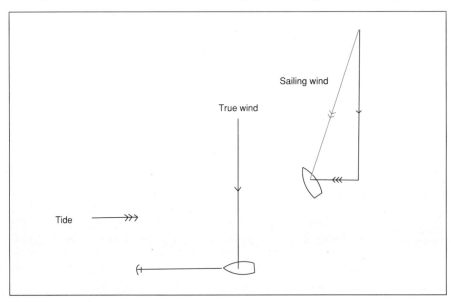

Obviously the effect of the stream will decrease as the ground wind speed increases. A two-knot tide has much less effect on the wind speed if the ground wind was 30 knots to start with. However, even in these stronger winds the tidal wind may be worth considering, and a change in the wind speed from 28 to 32 knots is still not insignificant.

Because the sailing wind is affected by so many factors with the tide being merely one of them, it is not often worth trying to calculate the changes which will occur on the turn of the tide exactly. In most cases it is sufficient to understand the concept and use approximations (such as the 1-in-60 rule) for the calculations. However, in very light winds and strong tidal streams the overall effect of the tide is so great that it can be worth attempting to work out the changes somewhat more accurately. In these cases a double triangle as shown in diagram 29 is the easiest way to resolve the question.

In longer-distance races especially, it can be useful to keep a check on the wind strength and direction in order to forecast the weather more accurately. If you are attempting to do this, it is most important to remove the effect of the tidal stream from your calculations otherwise the whole picture of what is happening to the wind will be distorted. Just remember that it is the ground wind to which the weather forecasters are referring and not your sailing wind.

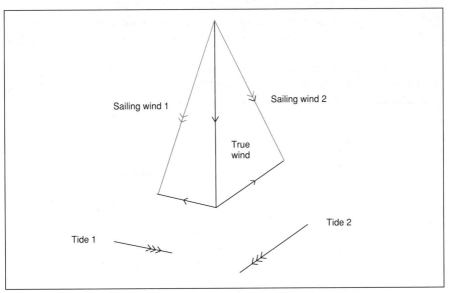

Sailing wind 1

Sailing wind 2

True
wind

Tide 2

Tide 1

29 Sailing wind changing with the tide

It must always be remembered that it is not just as the tide changes that differences in stream are encountered, but also when you go from sailing in an area of slack water out into the strong current or anywhere else that there will be a change in stream rate or direction. Diagram 30 shows a classic example: the tide inshore

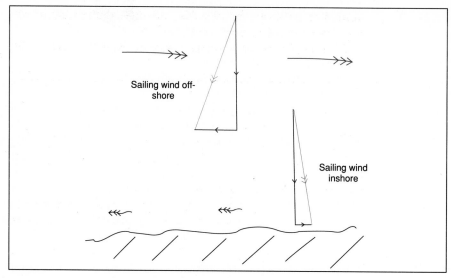

30 Sailing wind - in and out of the tide

is often slacker than that in the channel and may even have turned as in this case. Thus the sailing wind will be quite different depending on where you are sailing at the time.

What is VMG?

3.4 VELOCITY MADE GOOD (VMG)

VMG is a concept used primarily when beating upwind or running downwind and describes the compromise between the speed of the yacht and her pointing angle. To be literally correct the phrase should finish with VMG . . . upwind or . . . downwind, but in most situations it is not necessary to be so precise.

The easiest way to explain the concept is to look at a simple graph as in diagram 31 where boat speed and wind angle are plotted against each other. If the hypothetical yacht is travelling

31 VMG upwind

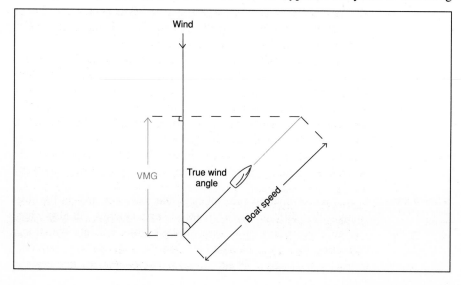

upwind at six knots and is making an angle to the wind of 45°, her VMG straight upwind would be 4.18 knots.

Diagram 32 shows a similar situation with the yacht going downwind.

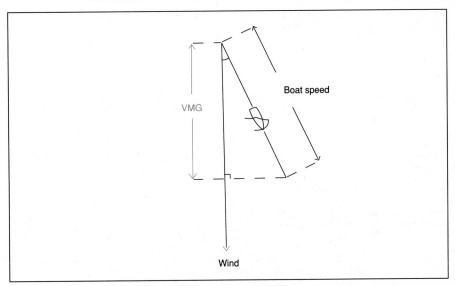

32 VMG downwind

From these diagrams it can readily be seen that VMG must be a compromise, if the yacht sails faster upwind by bearing away a little, then the increase in speed needs to at least make up for the extra distance sailed before it becomes a worthwhile exercise.

Practical use of VMG

If one's yacht has a dial giving VMG as part of its instrument system, as most will have nowadays, it would seem logical for the helmsman to steer upwind so that VMG is maximized. Let us look at this in a bit of depth and see if it would really work; initially we will look at the situation upwind.

The yacht is sailing along in a straight line at six knots with a wind angle of 45° and this therefore gives a VMG reading of about 4.2 knots. The helmsman tries pointing a little higher and, because of the inertia and momentum of the yacht, initially this gives a smaller wind angle without the speed dropping, thus the VMG increases. The helmsman thinks 'this is good, let's have some more of that' and points even higher. The same thing happens for a while even though by this time the sails are flapping. Eventually though, the boat speed will start to drop and VMG will come down again. At this point the helmsman would probably try to bear away in order to get VMG to rise, but this time the inertia of the yacht prevents her from accelerating immediately, so as he bears away the VMG drops even further . . . get the message?

The mirror image of this would obviously happen when sailing

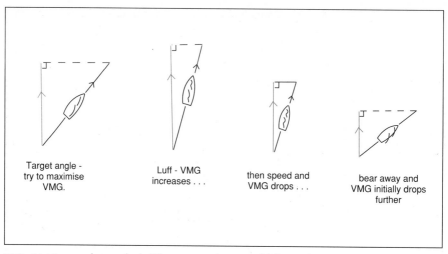

Target angle -
try to maximise
VMG.

Luff - VMG
increases . . .

then speed and
VMG drops . . .

bear away and
VMG initially drops
further

33 Don't let the
helmsman see
VMG

downwind. The temptation would be to bear away to a dead run in order to increase the VMG temporarily, but in the long term it could not work.

This shows that VMG cannot be used as a helmsman's tool, but it does not negate the value of VMG. If the VMG readout is placed where the trimmers can see it but the helmsman either cannot see it at all or is well conditioned not to look at it, then VMG can be a really useful tool. Now the trimmers can try a particular setting and allow the helmsman to settle down over a 30-second period or longer until boat speed and VMG have more or less stabilized. Then the trim of the sails can be altered slightly and VMG watched - if the new trim gives an average gain in VMG then it was good, if the effect was a lowering of VMG then whatever had happened to the boat speed or pointing angle cannot have been as good a compromise as it was before.

So, VMG is a trimmer's tool and not one for the helmsman to use. However, even as a trimmer's tool it does have severe limitations. The chief of these is that in order for it to be of any use, the wind strength must stay constant otherwise it raises the question of whether a change in VMG was caused by the alteration of trim or by the wind change.

Concept of target speeds

**3.5
TARGET BOAT
SPEED**

As has been seen in the previous section, VMG in itself has some uses but also serious limitations. Target boat speed is one way of utilizing the concept of VMG while getting rid of the problems associated with inertia and changes in wind speed.

The principle of target boat speed is that for any given wind speed there will be an optimum angle to the wind both upwind and when running, and that this optimum angle will also give one optimum boat speed. If in these same circumstances the boat

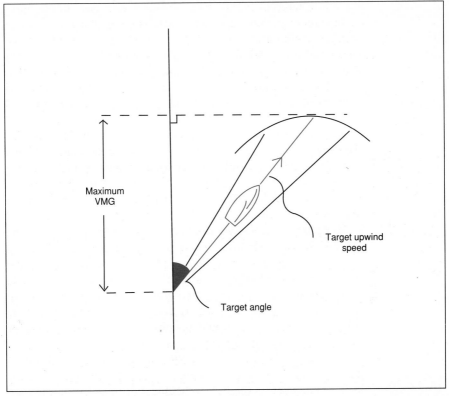

Maximum VMG

Target upwind speed

Target angle

34 Target speed and angle - upwind

speed is too high then, almost by definition, the angle must be too great if going upwind and too small if running.

Use of targets

Because the targets are linked inextricably to the wind speed, both need to be looked at together, but if this is done then targets can become both a trimmer's and helmsman's tool. Once again it is easiest to look at a realistic example to demonstrate how the system works in practice.

Using the table of target speeds and angles shown in diagram 35, assume that you are sailing along in eight knots of true wind with a boat speed of 5.9 knots and a wind angle of 40°, when the wind increases to 12 knots. The target speed for 12 knots of wind (from the table) is 6.4 knots, so the present speed is too slow.

The instinctive reaction for most people in this situation will be to luff up in the gust, but the use of targets will demonstrate that this is the wrong approach, at least initially. Since the boat speed will be below the new target, the correct procedure will be to bear away a little in order to accelerate until the new target speed is reached. At this point it will be possible to head up again while maintaining the new target speed. (This assumes that there are not any control problems in the gust when other factors may override the use of targets.) In this way, the best use is made of the gust.

In another example, the same yacht is going along in the same starting conditions of eight knots of breeze with 6.2 knots of boat speed and a true wind angle of 45° when she runs into a calm patch with a new wind of only four knots. At four knots of wind, the table shows that the upwind targets should be 3.7 knots of boat speed and an angle of 50° so the yacht is sailing too high and too fast.

Once again the instinctive reaction will be wrong. In this case the sails will actually go aback since the apparent wind will have gone forward quite significantly and the temptation will be either to bear away or tack 'on the header'. In fact the wind in this instance has not changed direction at all so tacking is not the right thing to do anyway.

Using target speeds, we would luff up in order to get rid of the 'excess' speed, even if this made the sails flap a little more. As soon as the speed started coming down towards the new target two things would happen. Firstly the apparent wind would move aft of its own accord and secondly we would bear away to maintain the new target speed. If the wind drop was a large one (relatively speaking) it would possible to gain a boat length or more every time this procedure was carried out.

The same principles apply when running downwind. If a light patch is experienced, the tendency will be to luff up to fill the sails again, whereas the best technique will be to bear away onto a squarer run until the excess speed has been used up and then luff up. Similarly, if a gust is experienced the first reaction should be to luff slightly in order to accelerate then bear away, rather than to bear away immediately.

Displaying targets

There are two basic ways to display target speeds and angles. The first and most sophisticated way is to have a set of complex instruments which contain a computer with a look-up table of targets in its memory. These instruments can then continually monitor wind speed and thus display the appropriate target speed and angle. This system works well and is to be found in the top-end racing instrument systems such as those produced by Brookes & Gatehouse or Ockam.

A simpler and cheaper method of displaying target speeds and angles is to write them down in large numbers somewhere where everyone can see them easily. Because they are likely to be updated fairly frequently as more information becomes known, the writing should be removable - I have found that a couple of strips of ducktape make an ideal writing surface on the aft end of the coachroof, or somewhere similar. Diagram 35 shows the sort of table which is required.

TRUE WIND SPEED	UPWIND		DOWNWIND	
	ANGLE	SPEED	ANGLE	SPEED
3	60	2.8	110	2.3
4	50	3.7	125	3.2
6	48	5.1	135	4.0
8	45	6.2	148	5.4
10	42	6.4	155	6.1
12	39	6.5	162	6.9
16	39	6.7	165	7.8
20	41	6.8	170	8.1
24	41	6.8	175	8.2
30	44	6.9	180	8.5

Obtaining target speeds and angles

This subject is covered in chapter 6.

4   Preparation

In my view adequate preparation is one of the prime factors in making a good racing navigator. Some of this preparation will be almost subconscious but a lot of it will involve hard graft and will take time, especially if sailing in a new area.

The more that can be prepared before the start of a race the better. Anything which can have been done or thought about beforehand leaves that much more time for thinking and considering the available strategic options while afloat rather than struggling to keep up with the minutiae of everyday navigation.

The good navigator will consider all aspects of his job: are the instruments calibrated? has he got all the charts? what are the tides doing? how about the likely weather forecast? and so on. This chapter considers the specific requirements of some parts of this long list, not all items on the list will be needed for all races, but all should be considered even if only for a moment.

4.1 PREPARATION EQUIPEMENT AND CALIBRATION

This is not intended to be a buyers' guide and indeed a book of this nature would be out of date even before it was published it if tried to fulfil that function. The purpose of this section is to consider what equipment is required, not who should be the manufacturer.

Plotting instruments

Some sort of plotting instruments are obviously needed, even if you also have full electronic systems. There are myriad designs and makes of plotting instrument and most work well for someone. My criteria for this are that it must be simple to use anywhere, it must be fairly robust, it must not rely on compass roses which are printed on the chart (they are never in the right place!) and ideally it should be possible to plot equally easily in degrees true or magnetic. My own preference at this time is for the Breton plotter as shown in diagram 36.

This has long enough sides to obviate the need for any other straight edge, it has its own compass rose together with a system for dealing with variation, and fulfils all my other requirements.

Any device which requires two hands or a flat surface for use,

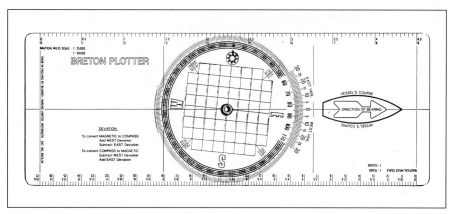

36 Breton plotter

should in my view be thrown away and that includes traditional parallel rulers and pairs of triangles. They may have a place where there is a proper chart table, but are of limited use on the side deck.

Measuring device

One of the advantages of the Breton plotter is that it has scales down the edges, either actual scales to relate to minutes of latitude on certain scaled charts or simple measurement in centimetres or inches. In most cases I prefer to have the latter since it is rare for Sod's law to provide you with a chart of a scale corresponding to those on the plotter.

If your plotting instrument does have a measuring ability then this can be very helpful in all sorts of ways, but even if this is the case you will probably still need some dividers. It is possible to get either straight or single-handed dividers and once again which to chose is a matter of personal preference. My own choice is for the straight type of dividers because they are marginally easier to stow on my portable chart board.

Pencils

This may seem to be such an obvious item as to be hardly worth mentioning, but if so I must disagree. Pencils are obviously needed for most plotting and if using waterproof paper they write much better than most inks with no fear of smudging.

Pencils need to have reasonably soft leads (2B is probably ideal, although HB will do at a pinch) but not be too soft or they will need sharpening too frequently. Because of the hassle of keeping ordinary pencils sharp I nearly always use disposable propelling pencils. If using these, never have the type with the lead protected by a fine, pointed metal sleeve - these are incredibly painful when embedded in the palm of your hand!

It is also useful to have a supply of Chinagraph pencils for temporary writing on smooth surfaces as well as some spirit-based markers for permanent writing on the deck, etc. On most boats I seem to be the only one always to have a marker in my pocket when required and I have found it necessary to label them to avoid loss.

Hand-bearing compass

The hand-bearing compass is another essential piece of personal kit. Some people like the electronic type of compass while others swear by one make or other of traditional magnetic compass. As long as it can be easily read by day or night and has adequate damping, this choice is best left to the individual.

My only definite criteria are that the hand-bearing compass must be small and strong enough to live either in my pocket or round my neck and I must be really familiar with it before I use a new type for racing. I have had my own mini 'Opti-compass' for years and find it hard to get the same results from other models, although I realize that this comes from familiarity rather than a superior mechanism.

Binoculars

The best binoculars I ever used were on loan to the British team from British Aerospace during the 1983 Admiral's Cup series. These were a gyro-stabilized set as used by helicopter observers in anti-terrorist situations. They were superb quality, with excellent optics, a magnification of about x 10 and the gyro to hold the image completely still regardless of the movement of the yacht. After a bit of practice it was easy to read the sail number on a competitor at over $1/2$ mile range. Their only drawback was that after about 30 seconds' use I suffered from extreme motion sickness due to the confusing images reaching my brain from my eyes and my balance mechanism. Their other problem was that after the series was over we were told that they cost in the region of £20,000!

In the real world, where this sort of equipment is still too expensive to be considered, I favour a small, almost pocket-sized pair of binoculars for general use, even though a large object lens will gather more light and thus be better in marginal light conditions. This is because I find the smaller types of binocular easier to stow and less tiring to use, so they will tend to be at hand while the more traditional 7 x 50s are still down below.

Unless you are prepared to keep scrapping one pair after another as soon as salt water gets inside, it is worth investing in a reasonably good, waterproof pair in the first instance. The best waterproofing seems to come from gas-filled types which positively prevent the ingress of any water or water vapour. With all binoculars it is important to rinse any salt from them as soon as possible after use to prevent this eating into the lenses or case.

Many makes of binocular are now available with an in-built bearing compass, which can make a big difference in taking bearings on distant objects - especially for someone as short sighted as myself. Some also have a grid which can be used to give an idea of distance off, providing you remember the scale used in your pair.

My current favourite as a combined tool is the KVH Datascope which has a good-quality monocular, well-damped electronic fluxgate compass and a very useful rangefinder all in the same chunky, pocketable case. I am still saving up to buy one (they cost several hundred pounds) and no doubt something else will have appeared on the market before long.

4.2 PREPARATION - PERFORMANCE DATA

Performance monitoring is covered fully in chapter 6. It is vital that as much information about the performance of the yacht is recorded at every opportunity and is then collated for later use. This information can be in many forms, from simple knowledge of basic boat speeds, through to an appreciation of target speeds and angles and ultimately as far as full speed polar tables for use either in diagrammatic form or within an on-board computer.

4.3 PREPARATION - PERSONAL

As well as getting all the equipment prepared it is very important that you, the navigator, are also really prepared. I hate going into a race where I feel harassed or where I have not done enough prior to the race and therefore I am under unnecessary pressure.

I like to be out on the race course early, preferably before most of my competitors, with no basic work still to do just prior to the race so that I have time to look at the conditions and get a feel for the day. In short, I like to use the pre-race time to get mentally relaxed rather than panicking about some minor detail or other.

This is not to say that I don't make good use of the time, but more that I like to feel that all possible preparations have been completed.

How many charts are necessary?

4.4 PREPARATION - CHARTS

One of the first considerations the navigator needs to make is whether the yacht has adequate charts for a particular race. What comprises an 'adequate' chart folio is always a matter of personal choice, but it is a question which always needs to be considered.

My own view is that in most situations it is advisable to have a copy of all the charts covering the race area, especially for shorter races where this does not involve very much expense. As an example, when racing in the Solent area I like to have the following charts:

a) plastic-covered 'racing' charts especially for inshore series;

b) overall chart of the Solent and Isle of Wight, 1:75,000 scale;

c) charts of the Western, Eastern and Central Solent, 1:20,000 scale;

d) charts showing the approaches at each end of the Solent, 1:20,000;
e) Very large-scale harbours and anchorages charts of the East and West Solent, most of which are unnecessary but a few containing really detailed chartlets of useful areas. The charts are to various scales, but the majority are 1:5,000.

This gives a chart folio for the Solent (an area about 25 miles long) of some eight Admiralty and three racing charts which probably seems excessive to some people. In my view though, all those charts are available and altogether can give a little more information than would be possible with only, let's say, the overall 1:75,000 scale chart. In another area there may only be a small-scale chart which would have to be adequate, but not ideal.

If considering slightly longer races where the full chart folio might run into several dozen charts then both cost and weight start to come into consideration and the following principles should be adhered to:

1. Certainly a chart showing the whole area of the race is good, although in really long races it may be better to split the course into separate legs and have a small-scale planning chart for each leg instead of for the whole race. For the average weekend offshore race this may mean a chart of about 1:250,000 or 1:500,000.

2. Medium-scale plotting charts are then needed in order to keep a reasonably accurate idea of your position. Depending on the race, these may be of about 1:150,000 or even 1:75,000. These would be the most used charts in the whole folio and if no headlands were reached while against the tide it may not be necessary to have anything of much larger scale. If it is necessary to go close inshore to cheat the worst of the tide, more detailed charts will also be needed.

3. Detailed charts for critical areas of the course are also required just in case they are needed. Headlands, areas of coast where it may be important to be able to sail close inshore and other similar areas should, if possible, be covered with charts of at least 1:75,000 and ideally even larger scale. If you consider that at this scale one mile is only represented by about three centimetres and when you then consider that it may be useful to think of going within a couple of boat lengths from a danger in order to get the most advantage, it can be seen that even 1:75,000 is not a very large scale; 1:20,000 or 1:50,000 can give significantly more detail.

As an aside, when looking at charts it is always worthwhile to look at the source data to see both when and to what scale the original surveys were carried out. If the last survey was carried out some years ago and the bottom is sand or shingle, you would have to treat the area with considerable caution. Similarly, if the largest scale survey was not of at least 1:10,000, it would be unreasonable to expect every single rock and danger to be marked.

Order charts early

If the yacht does need any additional charts then it is a good idea to order them as soon as the need has been realized. Although it may seem sensible to leave this until the last possible moment in order to have the most up to date charts available, this always leaves the possibility that the chart agent will be out of stock of that critical chart when you finally do order it. This is especially likely if taking part in a major race when a large proportion of the fleet will be ordering the same chart and the agent's supply, which seemed quite adequate for normal purposes, suddenly gets decimated.

Another reason for getting the charts in plenty of time is the slim chance that the chart may actually be out of print for some reason if you leave it too late. During the summer of 1979 parts of the British hydrographic service were on a 'work to rule' and certain charts were either not available or were only obtainable without colour printing - if you have ever looked at a metric chart with no colour then you will appreciate just how difficult they are to read and comprehend. This made the navigation on the disastrous Fastnet Race of that year even more difficult than it would have been otherwise.

Chart corrections

Whatever type of charts you favour using it is imperative that they are kept up to date. In the UK it is possible to get weekly notices to mariners in order to do your own chart corrections, although for most of us this is probably taking things a bit far. As well as producing the weekly notices, the Admiralty also publish a quarterly notice for home waters which is probably adequate for most corrections.

However frequently you are prepared to do chart corrections, it is worth getting into a habit so that they get done on a regular basis. It is also important to look out for new editions of the charts in use since these might mean that several large corrections have been done at once and not necessarily promulgated under the notices-to-mariners system.

With racing marks whose positions seem to change quite often without the authorities' knowledge, I always like to check their positions with GPS or Decca whenever I round them and compare their actual positions with those marked on the chart and update the chart if necessary. At the same time as doing this it is of course possible to update your list of waypoints, either in the machine itself or in your little black book.

Take charts home

One hassle which I am prepared to undertake on any yacht where I am the regular navigator, is to take the charts home at the end of each race rather than leaving them on the yacht.

This has several advantages, the first being that they do not stay damp in the chart table. It facilitates easy chart correcting, since this is a pleasant enough alternative to watching the television during the odd midweek evening and also means that you are able to plan properly for the next race rather than having to leave a lot of the preparation until you arrive on the yacht. The other major advantage is that the yacht never has unnecessary charts on board which can all add to the weight which is carted around the race course.

The only down side to the regular navigator taking the charts away each week is when, for any reason, he is unable to be with the yacht for a race. This could leave the stand-in navigator without any charts but in most cases, as long as everyone realizes that the charts are not left on board, this should not cause a problem.

When doing an inshore series which needs the same charts each week I rarely remove the charts since in this case it is not necessary and can prove more trouble than it is worth.

Additional grid/meridian lines

On small chart tables and even more for use on your knee while sitting on the side deck, having latitude and longitude scales around the edges of the chart is often not enough. Inevitably at least one scale will be unavailable when the chart is folded and often neither will be visible. I therefore copy the latitude and longitude scales onto most of the grid lines on the chart so that they are always visible. Done in small numerals with a fine, waterproof pen, this does not get in the way of any other plotting and makes life so much simpler.

37 Copy latitude and longitude marking onto grid lines

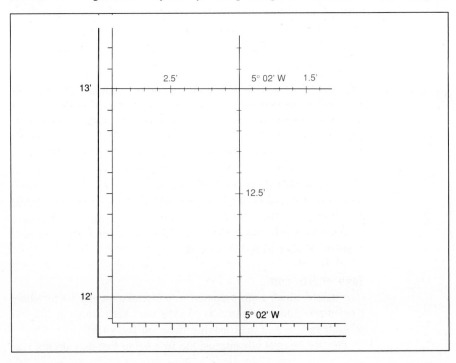

On some charts, especially really large-scale ones, I take this one stage further and draw additional latitude and longitude grid lines at one-minute intervals (depending on the scale of the chart) so that it is even simpler to transfer positions from the GPS onto the chart.

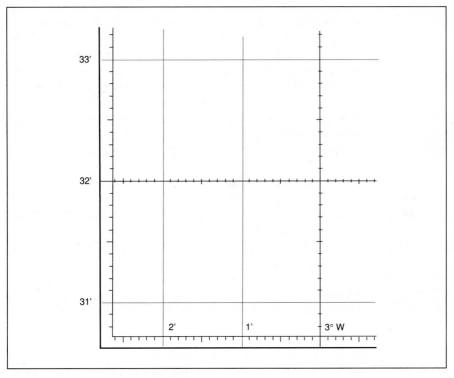

38 Additional grid lines make plotting easier

Immediately prior to a race

When I have the instructions for a particular race I like to get all the charts out and make sure that I have the right ones. If the course is known in advance, I then draw the straight rhumb lines between the various marks and write the bearing and distance for each leg on the chart. Although these lines give you a useful idea of the course, they can sometimes have too much influence over where you want to sail. My advice is to use such lines as a guide but treat them with caution and beware of convincing yourself that you must stay on them.

Another small task which I like to do is to mark on each chart, somewhere near the table of tidal diamond information, the times of high water for the appropriate standard port together with an indication of how 'neapy' or 'springy' the tides are on that day. This obviates the need to refer to any other bits of paper in order to use the tidal diamond information. Do remember to erase all this work at the end of each race because it is surprisingly easy to use old information at a later date.

The cruising yachtsman will usually sail with numerous books to help him with his navigation. On the modern racing yacht the list of necessary publications must be pared to the bone in order to save weight. In any case there should be little time for idle reading during a race!

Almanacs

One must have all the basic data required for a particular race: tidal heights, tidal streams, weather forecast times and frequencies, pilotage information for races which go close to a coast and so on. This information is generally all contained in an almanac (for example the Silk Cut Nautical Almanac in Britain), but invariably these are massive books which also contain reams of data which will not be required.

Whenever possible, I prefer to get the various books beforehand then extract the information which I require and copy it onto waterproof paper - so that I only carry the actual amount of paper which is required, maybe five or six pages from the almanac for a typical weekend race. Gathered together in either a loose-leaf folder or a 'floppi-file' (a book comprising 20-30 clear polythene envelopes used for display purposes) this makes an easy-to-reference file which is also light.

Manuals

As equipment gets ever more complicated it becomes more and more important to carry manuals and user guides on board. Such things as the GPS, Decca, yacht's instruments, etc. will probably all have functions and complications which are hardly ever used, but which will occasionally be required and it is valuable to be able to refer to a manufacturer's booklet when needed.

For longer races it is probably worth the effort to become better acquainted with the inner workings of at least some of these systems so that it would be possible to perform any user repairs while under way.

Racing rules

However well you and the rest of the crew know the racing rules it is impossible to know them all. This means that all racing yachts should carry a copy of the International Yacht Racing Rules on board, together with any prescriptions which are relevant for the race being undertaken.

Incidentally, always check in the sailing instructions which rules are being used and whether the prescriptions of a national authority are going to be in force since these can make significant differences.

A recent example comes from a Swan World Championship, held in Sardinia. The sailing instructions did not mention an advertising category and under the IYRR, as it was in 1990 this meant that it had to be a category A event and therefore not allow any advertising. As it was there were several Italian yachts which carried significant advertising and we decided to protest on a point of principle. Imagine our surprise when we were told that in Italy all racing was category B unless specifically mentioned in the sailing instructions. Our protestations that the event was not being run under Italian prescriptions were to no avail and we decided that it was not worth appealing against the decision.

If you are not really familiar with the racing rules, following a tip which I learnt from the Island Sailing Club at Cowes may help. Have a copy of the rulebook in the loo at home and read a little bit at every visit. You should soon find that your knowledge has improved.

As well as the rulebook itself there are various other books around which attempt to explain and interpret the rules and some of these are excellent and may well be worth adding to your Christmas present list. Do not forget that there is a major update of the rules every four years so that old books are completely worthless and should be disposed of to avoid confusion.

Basic tidal data

**4.6
PREPARATION –
TIDAL STREAMS
AND HEIGHTS**

Part of the information which I like to extract before the race from the almanac is the basic tidal data, that is the times and heights of high and low waters for all relevant standard ports. I have found over the years that it is all too easy to look up the wrong month or to apply local time-zone corrections the wrong way or to make any one of a dozen or so other stupid mistakes when extracting the information.

Doing the mundane job of getting the data from the almanac and onto a single sheet of paper is thus far better done at home, with fewer interruptions and while wide awake rather than on the side deck with the skipper screaming for information on which to make the next decision, with water pouring over the almanac and having had two hours sleep out of the previous 24 hours!

To decide on which standard ports are needed it is necessary to look at all the tidal stream atlases which are to be used and all the charts. If you think that the race should only take one day but might conceivably go on for three days, it is much easier to get all the data at one hit rather than having to start again halfway through the race. For some uses it will be important to extract the full information, heights and times for both high and low waters. For others only high waters will be needed - be selective in your choice so as to reduce the amount of work required and also to keep the data to a minimum.

For example, if you need the data for tidal stream use, then in most cases it will be necessary to extract the times of high water together with the tidal range and the mean ranges for springs and neaps. For local tidal heights, however, you would need all the information from the tide tables, together with corrections for the nearest secondary port.

Marking tidal atlases

Every page of each relevant tidal stream atlas should be marked up as part of the preparation for a race.

If the atlas is one of the Admiralty type then it should have the time for each day together with a 'springiness' or 'neapiness' factor (see chapter 2).

With the Reeves-Fowkes type of atlas, the relevant figure is the actual height of tide at the standard port (Cherbourg) so this should be included on each page. If the race is only going to take about a day, then a pencil line can be drawn alongside the appropriate column in the look-up tables on each page to make it even easier to extract individual rates or heights.

Tidal heights

Unless embarking on an exceptionally long race, I like to have worked out the tidal heights for all likely times and places as part of my preparation. For an inshore race in a known area this is no great hardship and may consist of the heights above datum at two or three places for the probable duration of the race, maybe a total of 20 or 30 calculations as shown for a typical Sunday race in the Solent in diagram 39.

14 July	0830	0930	1030	1130	1230	1330	1430	1530
Calshot	2.2	2.6	3.6	4.3	4.4	4.3	4.1	3.2
Solent Banks	2.0	2.4	2.9	3.4	3.3	3.2	3.0	2.2
Lymington	1.9	2.2	2.6	3.0	2.8	2.9	2.8	2.1

39 Example of inshore race tidal heights table

For somewhat longer races, the number of calculations can soon multiply. In the case, for example, of a cross-Channel weekend race, the difficulty is usually in deciding when your yacht is going to be close to a shore or danger for which heights are required.

The number of necessary calculations can be reduced if you consider the tidal stream direction at the same time as deciding where you may require to go close inshore. This is because it is obviously not going to be nearly as important to have good tidal height data if the tide is with you and the best strategy is therefore to stay in the deep-water channels. I have shown the sort of table which might be useful for a typical offshore race. In this case it goes from the Solent across the English Channel to the Cherbourg peninsular and then back again.

Friday	1900	2000	2100	2200	2300	2359				
Cowes	3.1	3.7	3.8							
Ryde		4.0	4.1	4.0	3.7					
Sandown			3.6	3.5	3.1	2.8				
Saturday	0700	0800	0900	1000	1100	1200	1300	1400	1500	
Cherbourg	2.2	2.3	2.8	3.7	4.6	5.2	5.3	5.2	4.6	
Barfleur	2.3	2.1	2.4	2.9	3.9	4.8	5.4	5.5	5.2	
Sat/Sun	1800	1900	2000	2100	2200	2300	2359	0100	0200	0300
Selsey	4.4	3.9	3.5	2.7	2.0	1.5	1.7	2.1	2.4	3.0
Portsmouth	3.8	3.4	3.1	2.2	1.6	1.6	1.9	2.1	2.4	2.8

40 Example of offshore race tidal heights table

In fact for races in the English Channel it is doubtful whether it is worthwhile to do a proper tidal height table of this kind as long as the yacht carries a copy of the relevant Reeves-Fowkes tidal atlas. It is so simple merely to look up the height of tide for a given place and time that extracting the data beforehand seems somewhat superfluous.

4.7 SAILING INSTRUCTIONS

Both the *Notice of Race* and the *Sailing Instructions* are vital to successful racing at any event. They contain all sorts of details about how the racing will be conducted and must be understood by all the principal people on the yacht if misunderstandings are to be avoided.

I feel very strongly, having learnt the hard way at various times over the years, that more than one person should read the instructions. Classic and well-documented cases of major blunders being caused by only one person reading the instructions have happened in the past and highlight my view.

Examples are *Blizzard* leaving West Lepe on the wrong hand during an Admiral's Cup inshore race, or myself losing first place in a RORC offshore race by not noticing that Bembridge Ledge buoy had been substituted for the Nab Tower between the notice of race (which I had read properly) and the sailing instructions (which I had only scanned briefly, 10 minutes before the start). This last mistake added about 12 miles to the race and *Marionette*, on which I was the navigator, went from an easy first to fourth. As we sailed towards the Nab Tower and saw the next two boats alter course some miles behind us to head for Bembridge I checked the course in the instructions. At this time it did occur to me that I could have quietly ignored my error, got off the yacht at the end of the race and then never spoken to any of the crew again - ever! However, after a few moments of reflection I chose the honourable route.

My policy nowadays is to read the instructions (and notice of race) through carefully, then read them again and mark any unusual or critical points with a highlighting pen before getting at least one other person on the yacht to read them. This second person often finds something of note which I have missed and spreads the responsibility wider.

If the course is being displayed just before the start I would also advise at least two people to take it down and check it. One lesson which I believed I had learnt some years ago but which was recently brought home to me, is that in these cases the committee are often allowed to change the course as late as the five-minute gun - so check the course after this just in case.

4.8 WEATHER FORECASTS

The importance of forecasts

Weather forecasts are very important to the racing navigator because in the end it is on the basis of his own interpretation of all the meteorological information that all strategic decisions are made. I also believe, however, that a large number of bad decisions are made on the back of inadequate forecasts, with the forecasts being blamed later.

For example, if you were beating on, say, a 60-mile leg and the forecast is for the wind to veer after about eight-ten hours as a front goes overhead, it would be a brave man who went too far towards that expected veer in the early stages of the beat in case the meteorologist's timing was wrong. If the beat was going to take, say, 12 hours, then it would only take a delay of a couple of hours in the passing of the front (or whatever) for there not to be a veer at all! On the other hand, if the beat was twice as long, then it would probably be reasonable and safe to make real use of the forecast since the front would almost certainly reach you in time to be of use.

In general it is safer to temper a belief in weather forecasts with caution, using the current conditions to best advantage whenever possible since short-term gains, once consolidated, are 'in the bag', whereas forecast gains may never happen.

Sources of weather information

There are many different sources of weather information. Some are more relevant to one situation than to another and some will tend to be more accurate than others. Most sources will have their use at some time and therefore need to be considered.

a) Shipping forecasts: Broadcast four times a day and covering the sea areas around the British Home Waters, these are some of the most detailed forecasts available on the ordinary radio. They give a general synopsis as well as area forecasts and actual weather reports and can be very useful for somewhat longer races.

The down side to this type of forecast is that it is normally for a 24-hour period, each sea area covers a large chunk of sea and the forecaster has a very limited time to give a lot of information. These factors mean that although good in a general way, these forecasts tend not to be very detailed and often need backing up from other sources.

One of the major plus points compared to a lot of forecasts is the inclusion of a general synopsis because from this it is possible to build up at least a basic picture of what is causing the particular weather and thus give a better understanding of how the weather may not concur with the 24-hour forecast if the underlying conditions change.

b) Local radio forecasts: These are broadcast at various times of the day by most of the local radio stations around the coast. Some, such as Radio Solent, provide detailed forecasts which are eminently suitable for sailing purposes while others tend to give much less useful information, more suited to tourist use than for sailing. The point is to get to know your local radio station, listen to the information which they are giving and see over a period of time whether it is likely to be useful and also decide for yourself if they are accurate.

Even forecasts which just give inland temperatures can be useful, especially when trying to decide if a sea breeze is going to set in, since you can compare the forecast land temperature with the known sea temperature and see if there is enough difference (at least two degrees centigrade and preferably four degrees centigrade) to get the sea breeze going.

For offshore racing these forecasts have the opposite down side to the shipping forecasts, they tend to be very coastal and may not extend far enough out to sea to give a full picture.

c) Coast radio stations: These normally just repeat the shipping forecasts and therefore do not offer anything new. However, they usually repeat the forecast at an easy dictation speed and do at least offer alternative times for the forecasts which may be more convenient.

d) Coastguards: The coastguards will often also repeat the local part of the shipping forecast and will sometimes give local conditions as well. This is becoming less and less usual as the coastguard service moves towards large control centres and away from small lookout posts.

If the sailing instructions allow it, you may sometimes be able to get good local information by radioing the coastguard and asking what the actual conditions are at the time. Beware though, in a lot of races this would constitute outside assistance and may lead to a protest against you.

e) Television: The forecasts on television are visual and are therefore quite easy for the less experienced meteorologists among us to understand. The problem in most cases, though, is that television is not available to us while sailing. Small, portable televisions make it possible to use this technology while in coastal waters but since it is really on longer races that the type of synoptic information available is most use, the usefulness is very restricted at present.

My view is that getting a good grasp of the general weather situation *before* the race is vital, and television is one good way to do this.

f) Newspapers: Most of the same comments made about television also apply to newspaper forecasts. They are good for getting a build up over the few days before a big race.

g) Weatherfax: On-board weather fax machines are coming down in price and can be extremely useful, especially for longer races. They provide up-to-date weather charts, both for sea level and the upper atmosphere and are a valuable supplement to other forecast sources.

For those who sail with a portable computer on board, it is possible to get software which puts the weatherfax information up on the screen, assuming that the computer is plugged into a suitable radio.

h) Local meteorological office: It is quite possible to arrange with your local meteorological office (or airport) to be able to call them and speak to a real meteorologist about the likely conditions during the race. With care this can be very useful and can give the most relevant information available - if you ask the right questions.

You do need to be aware that even this information is still only going to be based on the same data as all other forecasts rely upon, and not assume that it is going to be inherently more accurate. Once you get to know a particular forecaster, they will often become even more helpful and they will get to understand your own level of knowledge.

Even if you carry a portable telephone on the yacht, most races at present would not allow you to access information by actually talking to a meteorologist without considering it to be outside information. It is always allowable to get this sort of help up to the five-minute gun and I often telephone the met. office just prior to a start in order to get the latest update.

i) Recorded forecasts: The British met. office has allocated various numbers in the 0898 series to give recorded information for most parts of the waters around the British Isles. Since this is recorded and is freely available, it can be used while racing. In most cases, however, it does not give any more information than that given on the shipping forecasts.

j) On-board forecasting: However much data you are able to receive from outside sources, it is always down to the person on board to interpret this information. You should get used to keeping a record of the barometric pressure and looking at the cloud formations, etc., to assist you with this forecasting. Often the actual, local conditions will not match up exactly with the forecasts and you need to unravel the reasons and then do your own forecasting. Practice, together with an understanding of the principles involved, is the only way to succeed in this. There are many excellent books on the weather and forecasting which may help you get the understanding necessary, but most of it is down to hard work.

5 **Working On The Side Deck**

5.1
WHY NAVIGATE
ON THE SIDE
DECK?

When I first started navigating on racing yachts in the early 1970s it was still normal for the navigator to spend a considerable amount of his time down below beavering away over a chart table. Most racing yachts had a good navigation area with plenty of stowage and a comfortable seat.

The next stage was to see chart tables which could be tacked from side to side so that the navigator could always work on the preferred side while still staying down below for the majority of the time.

In recent years the tendency has been more and more towards side-deck navigation with only the occasional foray down below when absolutely necessary. Maxis and heavier cruiser/racers still have the traditional navigation area below but not many smaller racing yachts are so well equipped.

The necessity for staying on deck comes from the development of ever lighter yachts with the crew weight playing a bigger and bigger role in the overall stability of the yacht. In practical terms it has become easier to navigate on deck since the advent of paper-laminating techniques, position-fixing aids to reduce the amount of basic navigation required and so on. Apart from any weight consideration, the chief benefit of staying on deck as far as I am concerned is the degree of involvement that the navigator can have in the running of the yacht and his ability to look around and have an input to tactics and short-term weather forecasting.

Having said all the above, there are still times when some or most of the navigation is best done below. On big, narrow and heavy yachts, for example, your weight is unlikely to affect her performance. During a wet and stormy night at sea the compromises needed to navigate on deck may reduce accuracy to an unacceptable level. In light airs, especially downwind, it may even be better to have your weight below, as long as you do not then need to keep surfacing like a jack-in-the-box to look around.

5.2
WATER-
PROOFING
YOUR
EQUIPMENT

If you are going to be effective in your job and also work on the side deck, then most if not all of your equipment must be waterproofed. There is no point in pretending to set yourself up for on-deck navigation if you need to disappear below every time it rains or is rough.

Paper is the most commonly used material which normally gets ruined by water and therefore needs some work to be done on it before it is possible to use it on deck. There are several options open to you when considering how best to go about waterproofing.

Plastic envelopes

The simplest way to waterproof a piece of paper is to put it into a transparent plastic envelope. This works fine for single sheets, especially if they will only be used once, but tends not to be very effective in the long term. I like to have at least one 'floppi file' on board with maybe 20 or 30 plastic pockets for the insertion of such things as the sailing instructions and extracts from the almanac. In my experience, plastic folders are not ideal for charts since it is really difficult to hold the chart and the plastic together sufficiently to allow for plotting.

Laminating

Laminating is another technique which certainly has its place. It is ideal for small sheets which are going to be used over and over again, for example tidal stream atlases. There are two basic finishes available, either gloss or matt. The latter is less commonly available but has the advantage that it is easier to write on.

Although it is obviously possible to get full-sized charts laminated, in my experience they are too unwieldy for effective use on board. Once again, if a particular area is being raced in a lot, it is possible to cut the relevant bit off a full-sized chart and get that piece laminated.

Paper waterproofing lacquer

Lacquer has been used for years by mountaineers and hill walkers to waterproof their maps. It is available as a spray from some good chandlers or from any specialist mountaineering shop. The spray helps to protect paper and makes it last many times longer than normal but it does not give the protection of lamination. The chief advantage of lacquer is that it does not make the paper any more difficult to fold or handle and you can use ordinary pencils and erasers.

One word of warning - the lacquer has a high solvent content and it is vital to allow the paper to 'air' thoroughly after treatment before taking it on board or anyone down below with the charts will end up somewhat high!

Waterproof paper

Truly waterproof is available either in notebook form from most chandlers or in larger sheets and as special paper for photocopiers from main distributors. This paper is not cheap but it makes writing on the side deck possible in all weathers. As well as the navigator having at least a notebook I believe that trimmers should also be equipped with the means to make notes at any time.

**5.3
PLOTTING
BOARD/
CHART TABLE**

If you are going to be effective as a navigator while on deck then you must be able to perform most of the functions that were previously done at the chart table below. This means that in a lot of cases you will need to have a flat surface for resting your charts on to enable you to plot courses, positions and so on.

It is just about possible to utilize the side deck itself as your flat surface in light conditions (and if the side deck is wide) but once the wind gets up and the spray starts flying this becomes too difficult and a custom board of some kind becomes essential.

Over the last few seasons I have gradually developed my plotting board from its beginnings as a simple clipboard. My present board comprises, as shown in the diagram, a piece of marine plywood 400mm x 600mm. This has a clipboard clip screwed to its top edge and two lengths of shockcord going around it. These hold the charts in place regardless of the weather. The reverse side has a navigator's briefcase attached to it which enables me to have ready access to my plotting instruments, tidal atlases, sailing instructions and so on.

The back of the board is painted white which allows it to be used as a noteboard for plotting the relative positions of the opposition or other notes as required. Either a very soft pencil or a Chinagraph marker works well on this surface.

41 Portable
plotting board

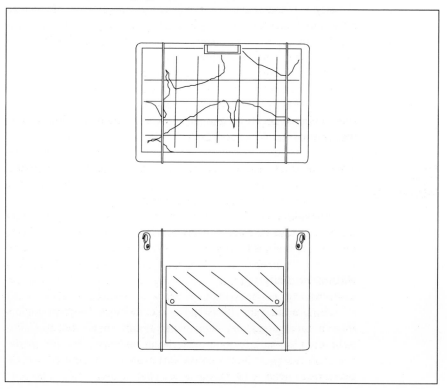

In addition to the above, there are also hooks on the two top corners for clipping it to the guardrail. This enables me to leave the board on deck but secure when it is not needed and also allows me to work with both hands with it on my lap while sitting out on the rail. I used to use plastic hooks until one time when the board got caught in the runner during a gybe and the hooks both distorted and I lost my board. I now use small stainless spring hooks (Wichard or similar).

5.4 WORKING AT NIGHT

Navigating on the side deck at night adds another dimension to the difficulties of the job. Effective lighting is essential but it must not dazzle the rest of the crew. I use a combination of different lights depending on exactly how much light I need.

My main light for doing complex plotting or reading/writing tasks is normally a cavers headlamp. These are torches attached to a simple harness for wearing on your head. They leave both hands free for working and provide light exactly where you are looking. Their chief disadvantage (apart from looking strange in daylight) is that you must be very disciplined not to look around at other crew members with the light switched on or you will ruin their night sight.

For the times when a very dim source of illumination is required, I use a Beta light. These were originally developed for military use and provide a dim green glow, just enough to read by at close quarters. They are quite expensive to start with but require no batteries and last for years. For general use I also always carry an ordinary small waterproof torch.

In the past I have tried a car map reading light with a clip to attach it to the edge of my plotting board, but although this looked perfect when trying it ashore I found it made the plotting board too cumbersome afloat and in any event could not find a fully waterproof version of the light.

5.5 PLOTTING INSTRUMENTS

Which plotting instruments are best tends to be a very personal choice. Some people swear by one particular instrument while others wouldn't go to sea without another.

Although parallel rulers have their place on large, stable chart tables, I believe that they have little use on your knee while sitting on the side deck. Whichever actual brand of instrument you prefer it must be capable of transferring lines to and from the chart accurately, easily and quickly. Ideally you should not need to use a second instrument (such as a ruler) for drawing at all.

Sailing around the UK waters, where I do most of my racing, there is nearly always magnetic variation to worry about and I like to do my plotting directly in magnetic. This means that I normally use instruments which enable variation to be applied by the instrument, rather than having to do an arithmetic conversion first.

My favourite is the Breton plotter which seems to be as simple as possible, fairly sturdy and long enough along its longer axis to be able to draw most lines. For those who prefer to work on the chart in true, the Douglas protractor takes a lot of beating.

As long as your plotting instrument has a scale along its edges it is not often necessary to use a pair of dividers. I find that in most cases using the side of my Breton plotter is a simpler way to measure distance or transfer latitude and longitude positions than with a pair of dividers. However, there are times when dividers are handy and they are one of the items of equipment which I keep in my navigator's case.

5.6 ACCESS TO DATA

There is no point trying to navigate on the side deck if all the data which you require is down below. You must have easy access to the position-fixing data (GPS, Decca or Loran) and to the basic navigation functions on the yacht's electronics, such as log, D.R., etc.

If the yacht which you are sailing on is set up so that the navigation instrumentation is all down below, then it is probably better to arrange to do your plotting there as well. In the ideal world you would get the instruments moved or duplicated but that may well not be feasible or economically justifiable. The worst situation is to try to compromise so much that you are 'pretending' to navigate on the side deck but do not have the data to do an effective job.

Even though there are often very real advantages to navigating on the side deck, there will be other times when doing the work down below makes more sense. One example of this would be at night, in rain and light winds when your weight is not needed on deck and it is so much easier to work where it is relatively dry, light and comfortable. There are also some electronic navaids which are only splashproof and which cannot realistically be used on deck, such things as the Yeoman Plotter or electronic charts for example and the use of these may tempt you below in order to speed up the navigation processes. Do not get bogged down by thinking that you must always be on deck, use your common sense and do the job wherever is most sensible at the time.

5.7 SLEEP AND WARMTH

Lack of sleep and allowing yourself to get too cold are common but usually unnecessary accompaniments to offshore racing, especially when spending most of your time on deck. Both can dramatically reduce your mental efficiency and hence the performance of the yacht.

If you are going to get enough sleep then there are probably two totally separate ways that you will achieve this. The first will be to go down below for an occasional 'proper' sleep, in a bunk. This may not happen at all in a One-Tonner or similar, but on most cruiser/racers it is possible (and desirable) for some people to get real sleep whenever feasible. For the navigator to go below and sleep for two-three hours requires planning ahead to ensure that there is a spare bunk when it is convenient and sensible for him to go below. A reaching leg away from the coast is ideal since these normally require the least number of decisi . Other legs can be used for sleep, but you will need to brief ie crew very well as to what is required of them and under what circumstances you should be woken up.

The second way that you will be able to increase your sleeping time is to cat nap on the rail. With practice you should be able to get reasonably comfortable while sitting on deck - I find that as long as there is somewhere to rest my head then nothing else seems to matter. Cat naps of even a few minutes can revitalize your internal batteries and get your tired mind working again. It may be difficult to get much solid sleep but enough periods of five-ten minutes can give you most of the sleep that your body requires.

In order to sleep at all it is necessary to be reasonably warm. Even in summer I often wear a one-piece polar suit at night and nearly always wear some form of wet-weather gear at night to avoid getting damp with dew. If there are large waves throwing spray over the windward side deck then a hood to keep the worst of the water off will help your comfort enormously.

6   Performance Monitoring

It has always been important to keep a record of how a racing yacht performs, even before the introduction to yachting of complex electronic instruments and computers. There are several reasons for this, the first being nothing to do with racing but simply the ability to perform accurate navigation.

You must know more or less how fast a yacht will go in different wind conditions in order to be able to shape a course to steer. You must also know approximately how much leeway she will make, both for shaping courses and for plotting estimated positions later. For the purposes of cruising these need only be crude approximations, whereas for racing they need to be refined as far as possible, as we shall see later.

Even on the cruising yacht you need to know at what sort of wind strength to change sails and whether the yacht handles better with a reef tucked in the mainsail or with a smaller headsail. This is the start of sail evaluation.

While going along on a particular point of sailing it is nice, even while cruising, to know if you are making the best of those conditions. Apart from spurring you on to try harder, this also gives you an immediate indication if something has gone wrong, for instance if some weed has caught around the rudder.

These are some of the main reasons for wanting to monitor and record the performance of the yacht and this chapter will look at the subject in more detail.

6.1
SPEED POLAR
CURVES

Definition

Unless you are used to the terminology, 'speed polar curves' does not sound like anything very useful to sailors. All it means, however, is a graph to show the relationship between boat speed and wind angle for a particular wind speed and this is illustrated in diagram 42. This is merely a convenient way to represent and look at how fast a yacht will go in any given set of conditions.

The data is usually collated in tabular format to start with and it is in this format that it would be used by on-board computers. The graphical presentation merely makes it easier for a human navigator to interpret. An example of the tabular speed polar information is shown in diagram 43.

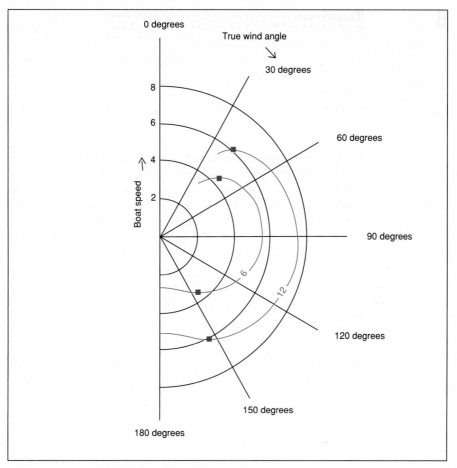

42 Speed polar curves

What data is required?

Before we get into the detail of polar curves it is worth going back a stage and considering what data about boat speed it is that we really want to obtain. In the perfect world we would have enough data to give us accurate 'best speed under normal circumstances' data for every wind speed and wind angle. In reality this would be a vast array of data which would take for ever to obtain and which would need a powerful computer to use.

In practice what is required is enough data to produce graphs at, say, three- or five-knot wind bands with the emphasis on the critical wind angles. By critical wind angles I mean those where a small change in angle or wind speed produces a relatively large change in boat speed - normally upwind, downwind and marginal surfing. In most cases, the changes in boat speed for other wind angles are not going to be very significant and it is therefore easier to produce an acceptably accurate graph from somewhat less data.

There are two ways in which a speed polar curve can be

65

represented. The easiest is to use apparent wind angles and apparent wind speeds plotted against boat speed. This is easier than using true wind because the apparent wind angles, being raw data, are likely to be quite accurate and are also more readily obtained using simple instrument systems. The problem with apparent wind curves is that they are not very useful, since one graph would represent a wide range of conditions of true wind and in any particular conditions it would be necessary to use a vast number of curves.

The more useful but also somewhat more difficult-to-produce figures are derived from true wind angles and speeds. This allows one graph to be used for one set of conditions, which obviously makes it much simpler to use.

43 Extract from a polar table

True angle	True wind speed		
	6	8	14
35	3.8	4.5	5.3
40	4.3	5.2	6.5
45	4.6	5.6	6.7
50	4.9	6.0	6.9
55	5.2	6.3	7.1
60	5.5	6.6	7.3
65	5.6	6.7	7.5
70	5.8	6.8	7.6
75	5.9	6.9	7.7
80	5.9	6.9	7.8
85	6.0	7.0	7.9
90	5.9	7.0	8.0
95	5.8	7.0	8.1
100	5.7	6.8	8.0
105	5.6	6.7	7.9
110	5.5	6.6	7.8
115	5.3	6.5	7.7
120	5.2	6.4	7.6
125	5.0	6.2	7.5
130	4.6	6.0	7.3
135	4.4	5.6	7.2
140	4.2	5.4	7.0
145	3.9	5.1	6.7
150	3.6	4.8	6.5
155	3.5	4.6	6.3
160	3.3	4.4	6.1
165	3.2	4.2	5.9
170	3.1	4.0	5.7
175	3.0	3.9	5.6
180	2.9	3.8	5.5

The difficulty of collecting data

Until a few years ago it was not really feasible to produce an accurate set of polar information; this was because by the time enough data had been collected to draw a curve the sails used to collect the data were worn out.

Even today, if the yacht does not have instruments which give a readout of true wind speed and angle, the calculations needed to convert from apparent wind into true would make the production of a realistic set off data totally impracticable.

The usefulness of VPPs

The necessity to collect vast quantities of data has been significantly reduced by the introduction of VPPs by most yacht design offices to give theoretical speed data for a yacht. All VPPs take the line, sail plan, approximate crew weight and so on and produce a set of speed polar information. Because it is only theoretical data being produced, it is possible to have sets of data for any wind speeds and any number of wind angles. Selected data from these tables can then be used to make polar curves for useful wind ranges.

International Measurement System (IMS)

IMS, which is one of the major handicapping systems in the world today uses a VPP as its basis. This means that any yacht which is measured under the system can obtain a set of speed polar data as part of the rating. This data will then be valid for other yachts of the same type and can be obtained without even needing the full measurement.

At present (1993) the IMS system uses a somewhat antiquated VPP and the figures which it produces are only accurate to within about 10-15 per cent, especially around the target areas upwind and downwind, but this lessens their value rather than removing all value.

Making real polars from theoretical ones

It is always much easier to modify some figures which are nearly but not quite correct than it will be to start from scratch and producing speed polar curves is no exception. If the starting point for a set of speed polar curves is theoretical data from a VPP, it has to be accepted that this will not in itself be totally accurate. It does, however, provide an excellent starting point from which to work.

As and when sailing in real racing trim, with everyone trying their best and concentrating hard, the actual speeds and optimum angles can be compared with the theoretical values. It may be that the actual speeds are five, 10 or even 15 per cent different at a particular wind angle and speed. The theoretical figures can be modified to include the new figures and the graph can be 'faired' to accept the new figures without major distortion as in diagram 44.

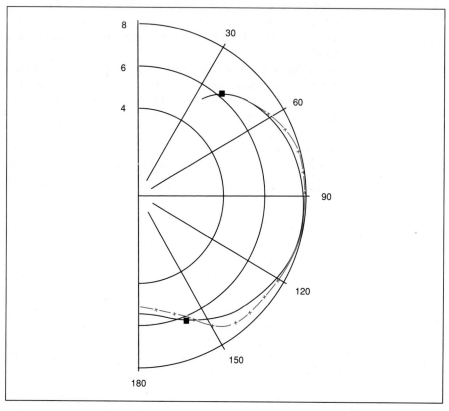

44 Use real data to 'fair' theoretical curve

Use of a computer with spreadsheet software is ideal for this sort of purpose since areas of the spreadsheet (the data) can be manipulated together without needing to alter each figure separately. On-board computers such as the Deckman also have the capability to hold and modify performance data in this way and can make life even easier (see chapter 7).

6.3 SAIL CHANGE CHARTS

As soon as there are more than two or three sails on board from which to choose it becomes necessary to have some organized way to ensure that the correct choice is always made. If a yacht always sails with the same crew then this is less important, but if, as in most cases, there are a variety of people sailing from time to time it becomes vital to have the sail selection system in writing.

At some wind angles and strengths, the choice of sail is obvious and little thought needs to go into a decision. At other times the choice is marginal; at the top end of one sail's range, for example, there will come a windspeed when the next sail down is faster and it is important to know just where that break point occurs. As the yacht bears away from close hauled to a close reach, a staysail might come into its own at one wind angle and then will come the decision of when to set a spinnaker . . . . These choices are often not easy and it frustrates me to sail on yachts where the break-even points have obviously been seen on many occasions but still no one knows or can quite remember what the angle was last time!

A fully formed sail change chart might look like the example in diagram 45 but there are obviously other ways in which the same information can be displayed. Do not worry if you are unable to fill in all the blanks, it is still worth starting to record the data as soon as possible.

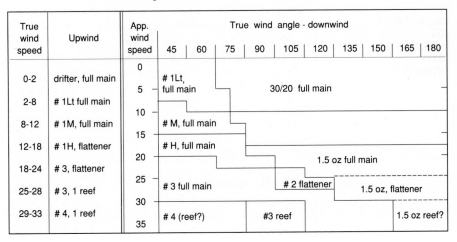

45 Sail change
chart

7   Sailing Instrument Systems

Why use instruments?

There is a school of thought which says that electronic instrument systems merely get in the way of real, seat-of-the pants sailing. This is not a philosophy of mine but in some circumstances it is probably a valid one. Used properly, instrument systems can enhance the ability of a good crew to understand their yacht and to get the best out of her and can make all sorts of decisions either easier or even just possible. It is doubtful whether even the best instruments will make a bad crew perform well; I believe it is important for a crew to learn the basics before they start to get involved in the use of complex electronics.

What are the basic requirements?

The single most important consideration with any instrument system is not which functions the system has or how big the displays are, but how reliable the system is going to be in the racing environment.

In the early days of Ockam instruments, I sailed on a flat-out racing yacht with the most sophisticated set of instruments imaginable (at that time) but we got little or no value out of the system because it was hardly ever working. I am glad to say that Ockam have come on a long way since then and are now some of the best systems around.

There must be local support for the system, however reliable it appears. Even the best will sometimes go wrong, or need re-configuring to link with a new fixing device, or something - and if there is no one locally who really understands the system it can be very frustrating to try to sort out what may in fact be a simple problem.

I experienced an example of this during 1991 when sailing on an Italian One-Tonner in the One-Ton Worlds. The boat had a new American GPS set (made by Trimble) which was supposed to output standard data in NMEA format. This was linked into a Brookes & Gatehouse 690 set of instruments and from there into a Deckman computer. Well, the GPS set gave perfect fixes on its own display but we could not get it to output a position to the B&G system. There was not a local service agent for the Trimble set and, although we tried all combinations that we could think of,

**7.1
INSTRUMENTS -
ARE
INSTRUMENTS
REALLY
NEEDED?**

70

the problem was not resolved until near the end of the championship when we finally got a reasonable output. It appeared that the Trimble set was not outputting NMEA sentences in a manner compatible with those expected by the B&G and we had to set up customized sentences and also switch the various instruments on in the correct order. Working in ignorance was certainly not bliss in this situation.

Simple necessities

The least that any racing yacht needs is a good steering and tactical compass, an accurate speedometer and an echo sounder (if sailing in shoal waters). These, plus a windex at the masthead and tell tales on the sails, will provide the bare essentials of information about boat speed, wind shifts and the like. For offshore racing this very basic setup should be augmented by a position fixer of some kind.

a) Compass: The compass needs to be readable to within two degrees, not for steering courses but rather for recognizing small wind shifts, especially upwind, while five degrees numbering is quite adequate for course steering.

Compasses can be either of the traditional magnetic type which is perfectly acceptable as a stand-alone unit or it can be an electronic compass, probably utilizing fluxgate technology. This latter route has the distinct advantage that the compass may be linked into an integrated instrument system at a later date, even if this is beyond the immediate budget.

Electronic compasses have other advantages as well. Most will give readouts accurate to within one degree and the compass itself can be placed anywhere on the yacht in order to minimize such errors as deviation, swirl and so on.

b) Speedometer: The speedometer must give an easily visible readout in tenths of a knot if subtle changes in boat speed are to be detected and a digital display is a great help for this. Ideally the speedometer should be capable of being calibrated so that it gives real speeds, but this is not essential unless two boats are being used for comparison.

c) Echo sounder: The echo sounder merely needs to be reliable and easy to see. Great accuracy is not called for in this department as long as the datum is known (that is whether it is giving readings from below waterline, below transducer or below keel).

In my view, echo sounders that give average depths over a variable time period are dangerous, especially if the switch for changing the period of average is easily knocked by mistake. Sailing with one such system, the time period for averaging could be varied from one second to 120 seconds and if one prominent switch was touched (for example with a knee) the display changed from one extreme to the other. This led on one occasion to us running firmly aground with the echo sounder still displaying a depth of over 20m - at least for the first minute or so of being on the bottom. Eventually, after 120 seconds, the display gave us the correct depth and showed that we were in fact aground.

d) Navaid: Navaids are covered in detail in chapter 8 but it is relevant to say here that for modern offshore racing an electronic position fixer is an almost mandatory piece of equipment which may link into the other yacht instrument systems or may be a stand-alone piece of equipment.

7.2 STAND-ALONE SYSTEM (SPEED AND WIND)

This section will look at the functions which are usual to find on systems which do not have any linking of data from outside the basic boat speed and wind instruments.

Boat speed and Log

As has been stated in section 7.1, the ability to measure boat speed is one of the functions which I consider to be an absolute essential for any racing boat. The associated function is the log which registers the distance travelled through the water.

Boat speed readout(s) must be available to virtually everyone in the crew and especially to the helmsman, tactician and trimmers. The navigator might need regular distance travelled information, so if on-deck navigation is being considered this must be taken into account in the positioning of displays.

Most people would agree that digital displays give an easier-to-comprehend readout of boat speed than analogue displays. An analogue display is excellent for giving an approximate idea of the value but for a racing yacht it is important to know the boat speed to at least the nearest tenth of a knot.

The damping of the raw boat speed data can make a display much more or less use depending on how it operates. The best systems will all have variable damping functions so that in calm water, the display might be showing virtually raw, undamped information while in rough seas it may be necessary to apply quite significant damping in order to stop the displayed information jumping too much. Most systems average the readings over a preset time period which could be anything from one to ten seconds depending on the conditions.

For the accuracy required at times when racing, the log (mileometer) needs to have a display accurate to hundredths of a mile. This allows sensible rounding of the last decimal place to be used and this then keeps the real accuracy for plotting to better than 100 yards.

The boat speed must be capable of being calibrated and ideally will have transducers mounted in such a way that accurate information is available at any angle of heel. Currently 'Sonic speed' as produced by Brookes & Gatehouse is the best system. This has one transducer mounted on the leading edge of the keel and another on the forefoot of the hull. In simplistic terms these measure the electrical resistance of the water between the transducers which changes as the boat speed alters. With no moving parts and transducers, which are a long way under the surface, this gives a very reliable system which is also extremely accurate.

If impellers or paddle wheels are used, they must be kept spotlessly clean and should normally be withdrawn after sailing each day. The average marina berth has a vast amount of fine sediment flowing past it and this can quickly wear out the impeller bearings and thus reduce accuracy. I always like to keep a spare impeller on the yacht in case the one in use gets damaged in any way and have found it useful to have a separate impeller system installed as a backup on a yacht with a sonic speed installation after the wire going to the keel transducer got damaged on one occasion.

Apparent wind angle

The apparent wind angle is one of the simplest wind functions and provides the basis of most other, more complex wind solutions. Typically it is measured with a wind vane placed near the forward side of the masthead.

On flat-out racing yachts, various experiments have been tried to ascertain the best possible place for the wind vane and it may be best to have it on a vertical stalk about a metre above the mast itself. The mechanics of producing a strong but very light stalk mean that most of us compromise and have the stalk, as in the first part of diagram 46.

46 Masthead units

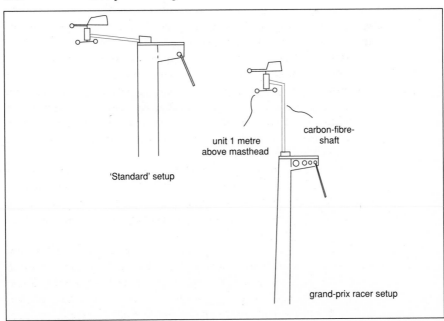

carbon-fibre-shaft

unit 1 metre above masthead

'Standard' setup

grand-prix racer setup

It needs to be understood that unless the vane is positioned completely outside the area of wind which is influenced by the sails, there will often be errors in the data due to both upwash from the sails and to the proximity of the unit to the masthead. The better systems will use some form of algorithms in their software to minimize these errors but obviously the cheaper systems tend not to do this. With some of the top range of systems it is possible to vary the corrections used in order to achieve the most accurate possible wind information.

Apparent wind speed

This is another of the primary functions in that it only uses data from one input source. This source is usually a set of rotating cups positioned just below the wind vane.

Calibration is covered later in this chapter. Suffice to say here that it is vital for any of the basic functions such as wind speed to be corrected as well as possible in order to minimize second-level errors in the more complex functions.

True wind speed and true wind angle

These outputs use a combination of apparent wind values together with the boat speed in order to solve the basic apparent wind velocity triangle.

47 True wind speed and angle

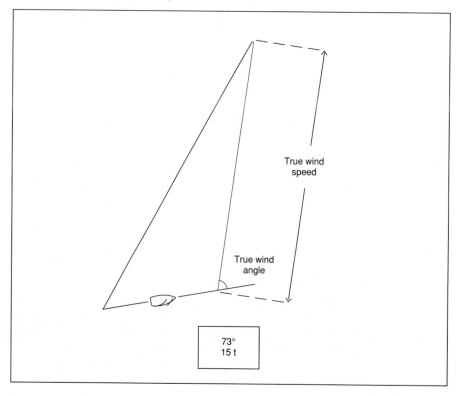

True wind speed

True wind angle

73°
15 t

Because they use a combination of inputs from three sources any errors in the base data may be magnified (or nullified) within the calculations. It must also be realized that there is bound to be a slight time delay between actually experiencing a change in the wind and this showing on the displays because of the processing time taken.

Assuming that the instruments are well calibrated, these outputs are some of the most useful since they give tacking angles and allow real trends in wind speed to be followed as well as giving a reasonable guide for when sail changes are needed.

Never forget that the wind being measured is that experienced at the masthead which is not necessarily the same as that applying to the sails. Unless there is good mixing of the air (due to convection) it is normal for the wind at the masthead to be faster than that lower down due to the friction of the surface.

Another point which is worth bearing in mind when using measured wind speed is that even if the anemometer is giving accurate numbers, the density of the air will vary with both temperature and humidity. Thus a wind of 15 knots may give totally different amounts of power depending on whether it is a hot summer's day (when the wind will tend to be less dense) or a cold day in the early spring (when the density might be 20 per cent greater). Never rely on wind speed as your only guide but use it with care.

Recognizing this problem, the team on the 1989 *Jamarella* 50-Footer attempted to use stress gauges on the rig and sheets to measure wind strength rather than simple anemometers. At the time this proved too difficult to achieve but it illustrates the level at which this problem is thought of in the upper reaches of racing technology.

Velocity Made Good (VMG)

As described in chapter 3 this is a combination of boat speed and wind angle for use when sailing either upwind or downwind (see diagram 48).

As a function it only has limited value since it cannot really take either changes in wind speed or the inertia of the yacht into account and therefore both lags behind the real world and also does not necessarily give a good idea of optimum speeds and angles.

Performance-linked functions

This function and the next (target boat speed) are included here even though they are more likely to be found in fully integrated instrument systems. They only rely on input from the boat speed and wind sensors but also need a fairly sophisticated internal computer which can contain and use look-up tables for either theoretical or actual performance information. These then allow

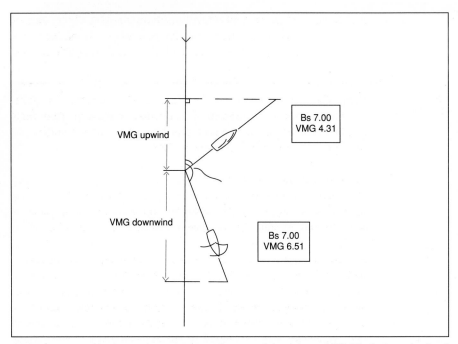

VMG upwind

Bs 7.00
VMG 4.31

VMG downwind

Bs 7.00
VMG 6.51

48 Velocity made good - VMG

the system to compare the actual speeds and VMGs being obtained against the theoretical values and give a performance readout, usually in the manner of a percentage.

If the data is based on theoretical performances, then your yacht is unlikely to be able to sail to 100 per cent capacity in all conditions. Sometimes it will be possible to sail faster than the hypothetical yacht and figures of 115 per cent or 120 per cent capacity may be obtainable, whereas at other times your yacht might be slower than the look-up table suggests and perhaps only 80 per cent or 90 per cent will be achievable. This does not matter as long as the crew get to know what sort of values to look for in the various different circumstances.

Because these are based on speed polar information (see chapter 6), they automatically take wind speed into account and can be a real help in monitoring the yacht's performance, especially offshore racing when out of sight of your competitors or when tuning up on your own. When using these functions beating or running, they still have the same time-lag problem that besets VMG.

Target boat speed

Once again the principle of target boat speeds was described in chapter 3. If an instrument system has the capability to give performance outputs as described above then it should also be able to output target speed information.

Having target boat speed displayed alongside the actual boat speed is probably the best way to ensure that the optimum speeds and angles are maintained when beating or running. As explained in the earlier chapter, target speeds get around the problems of inertia and time lags associated with any normal, VMG-derived function.

7.3 INTEGRATED SYSTEMS

Using the power of the silicon chip, it is possible to integrate complete systems. Combining the information derived from wind and boat speed transducers with that from the compass and/or the electronic fixing device (Decca or GPS).

Magnetic wind direction

This takes the wind triangle solution one stage further and combines the true wind angle (off the bow) with the heading of the yacht in order to give a value for the magnetic direction of the wind.

Naturally, if the true wind angle is not accurate along with a properly swung compass, the readout for magnetic wind direction will not be accurate either. Typically this output will change as the yacht tacks or as she luffs up or bears away. Various methods have been tried by different manufacturers to develop algorithms to correct the errors, but at present the best correction method is that contained within Brookes & Gatehouse's 690 system. Here there is a user-accessible look-up table where simple corrections can be input for different wind speeds and wind angles (upwind, reaching and running). This allows a simple but reasonably accurate correction to be made before the start of each day's racing - for the conditions at the time.

Having accurate magnetic wind direction is magic for the navigator since it allows him to track wind shifts on all points of sailing. In general terms, though, even a well-calibrated system will not be as good an indicator of wind shifts upwind as will the straightforward compass course. I find that when beating, the magnetic wind direction often gives notice of a shift which is about to make itself felt on the sails, while the compass heading shows the shift as it actually happens.

Obviously magnetic wind direction is actually showing the sailing wind since it will inevitably still include a tidal component (if sailing in a tidal stream). If it is necessary to ascertain the true wind direction, a simple velocity triangle will be required in order to remove the tidal vector (see diagram 49).

Dead Reckoning (DR)

If the compass is linked into the system then this is another very useful function. In basic terms, the instruments look at the distance run at the same time as the course steered to give a bearing and distance from the initial starting point which can be reset, for example, whenever a good fix is plotted. For traditional navigation this removes the biggest error which used to prevail namely that of the helmsman being honest in his estimation of the average course steered!

The other major use of this function which I have always believed to be under-utilized, is as a man overboard recovery aid. If the DR function is reset as the man falls in the water, then all that is needed to return to the position in the water where he fell in is to sail the reciprocal of the DR bearing until the DR distance is zero. Unlike man overboard functions on position fixers, this automatically takes current and surface drift into account (as long as the man is experiencing the same conditions as the yacht).

49 Magnetic
wind direction

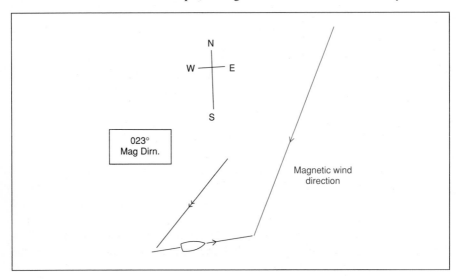

50 Dead
reckoning - DR

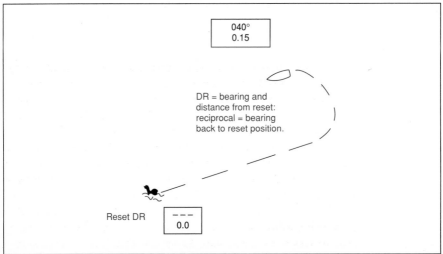

Next-leg wind data

Once the system is capable of computing the magnetic wind direction as you are going along, it is only a small step forward to enable it to solve the triangles necessary to display the wind on the next leg of the course. In its simplest form this output requires a manual input of the course to be steered on the next leg and the instruments then just solve the triangle as in diagram 51.

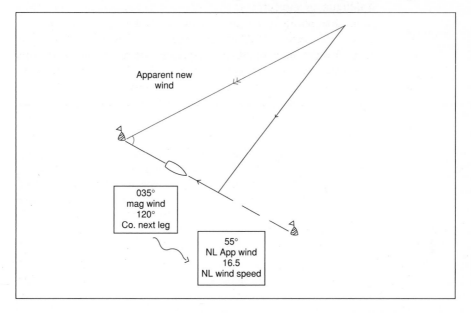

Apparent new wind

035°
mag wind
120°
Co. next leg

55°
NL App wind
16.5
NL wind speed

51 Wind on the next leg

In even more sophisticated systems, where the position fixer is also linked into the other instruments, it is possible to get the instrument system to give you the course to steer and the wind on the next leg having merely input the position of the marks as waypoints.

Tidal data

If the system knows the average course and distance sailed through the water via its DR function and also knows the course and speed over the ground from the position fixer, it is a simple enough calculation for it to work out the difference between these and output this difference as tidal rate and direction.

For this to give reasonably accurate information, the position fixer must be giving consistent fixes. It also helps considerably if the boat speed and direction are also consistent. With Decca or Loran sets it is normal to need at least four-five minutes averaging in order to remove the effect of the fixes jumping, whereas with GPS, if it is working well you may be able to reduce the averaging time to less than one minute.

My advice is to watch the tidal rates and direction carefully over a period of two or three minutes and only believe it if it stays constant. Even with GPS, it is probably not going to react fast enough to tell you when you have just gone into stronger (or weaker) tide while beating along a shoreline and will need some time on a steady heading in the new tide before it will give an accurate reading.

Analogue or digital?

Both analogue and digital displays have their place within any system. In general terms analogue displays are best for showing data where you need a quick and not particularly accurate indication of the data, while digital displays are better for that information where the actual numbers matter.

The comparison of digital versus analogue watches serves to illustrate this point. If you merely want to see an approximate time, say to within 15 minutes, then the analogue watch is quickest, whereas if the time is required more accurately then the analogue watch forces the wearer to interpolate between figures in order to reach an accurate answer. The digital watch on the other hand, makes it very simple to give a time of, say, 1611, but will require thought to convert that into a 'useful' time of 'about 10 past four'.

A 360° apparent wind angle indicator is one classic example of where the analogue display is easier to use than a digital one. It allows very rapid assessment of where the wind is relative to the bow or stern in the same way that a windex would, but it does not allow accurate estimates of the wind angle to be made. If using instruments to steer by, I would rather have the analogue display in this case, but if wanting data for navigation or sail-change purposes, the digital display would always win.

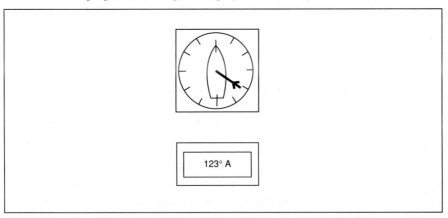

52 Apparent wind angle - analogue or digital?

Most other data is probably best displayed digitally, for example boat speed, wind speed, performance data, etc. With digital displays, the accuracy of the display is also important. There is a tendency for information to be displayed to unrealistic and unnecessary levels of accuracy. For example, with position fixers like Decca the real accuracy is likely to be to within 100m or so, while the display will usually give positions to the nearest hundredth of a mile (20m). This is fine as long as the user does not get the wrong impression of the actual accuracy and start using it as if the display must be right.

Single- or multi-function (MFD) displays

Some displays have one piece of information on them while others have several different items of data. Assuming that the crew need to have a certain number of functions on display at any one time, multi-function displays are obviously more cost-effective. The trouble with a multi-function display is that it is probable that the individual pieces of information are not going to be so easy to see as if they were shown on a dedicated display.

In my opinion, the most important thing to think about when deciding what type of display to use in a given situation is who will be using the information and whether it is going to be clear enough for them to read. The other consideration, especially if the instrument system is capable of outputting a great many different functions, is that unless it is possible to have sufficient dedicated displays for everything virtually any display should be able to be switched to show any function easily and quickly.

Mast display (20:20s)

For those of us who are short sighted, large-digit mast displays are a real boon. Even for normal-sighted people, they make it so much easier to see the important readouts that I believe any real racing boat should at least consider installing them. Having boat speed, wind angle and compass visible to all the crew at any time is a major plus.

If considering adding these jumbo displays into a system, beware slightly of which units you install since some use large amounts of power and many are not easy to see in some lighting levels.

Navigator's displays

When sailing on yachts which have been set up by other people, one of my chief complaints is not having ready access to all the data which my job as navigator requires - easily and without going below or getting off the side deck.

If as tactician/navigator you are going to be looking at wind shifts and call headers and lifts when beating, it is obviously vital that both the compass and magnetic wind direction are easily in view from your position on the boat.

If using a position fixer to give you waypoint information such as bearing and distance to the next mark then this too must be accessible. Ideally, it should also be possible to change which waypoint is being looked at without going below, although this is probably slightly less important.

If keeping track on the position by traditional means it is going to be necessary to have at least a readout of the distance run available, or preferably a display of the DR bearing and distance, together with a means of resetting it to zero.

When approaching a mark the wind calculations for the next leg are going to have to be done and here it is handy if all the information is available without having to make big efforts to get at it.

In all the above situations it can be seen that it is really important that the navigator has access to the required information whenever he needs it. If it is an effort to access a particular piece of data then it is likely that this will be skimped, guessed at or ignored altogether.

An example of this might be the wind calculations for the next leg. Ideally these would be done several times on the approach to the mark, ensuring that wind shifts and increases or decreases in wind speed are fully taken into account. However, if it is necessary to get off the side deck and go down below in order to access the required data, it is highly unlikely that the calculations will be done at all since a guess might be considered more acceptable than losing the navigator from the deck for several minutes. If he is allowed below once, it is even less likely that he will be allowed to go up and down several times.

In my view there are three acceptable solutions. The first is to have a large number of displays sited where everyone can see them so that any data which is required is available without too much of a struggle. This involves considerable expense and potentially a large drain on the yacht's electrical circuits as more and more power is used.

The second solution to at least part of the problem is to accept that a large proportion of the data is only going to be available at the chart table and to allow the navigation to be done from there. This obviously has the problem that crew weight is not being placed where it will do the most good. This is probably the best solution for relatively heavy cruiser/racers where crew weight is not too critical.

Probably the best solution is to have one or two dedicated displays at the back of the yacht where they are readily accessible by the navigator. One especially neat solution is to have these on a wandering lead so that they can be taken from side to side as required. With a Brookes & Gatehouse 690 system it is feasible to have just one MFD (plus ideally a waterproof position fixer) on a small board and then all functions can be accessed at will.

53 Mobile
instruments
on a board

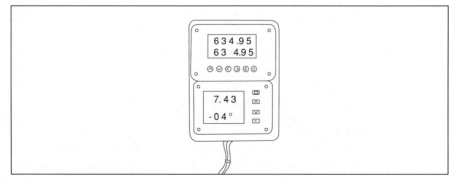

**7.5
CALIBRATION**

The importance of calibration has already been stated elsewhere, but it does no harm to stress it again here. There is no point in spending money on complex instrument systems unless the information produced is of a high degree of accuracy and the more complex the output, the more this is true.

The average cruiser/racer might, if the navigator feels particularly virtuous, do a calibration run for the log and a swing of the compass once a season. Compare this to an America's Cup yacht which will be doing the same thing at least weekly and which will be re-calibrating the wind angles and performance data on a continuous basis.

Boat speed and log

These are the most crucial of all instruments. The boat speed is used in nearly every secondary function and boat speed itself is vital as an indicator of performance, it is therefore most important that this is calibrated very early in any sailing programme and is then regularly checked for continuing accuracy.

The normal method of checking boat speed or distance run (which are usually inextricably linked within the system software) will be to do one or more timed runs over a measured distance. As with other calibration functions, the owners' manual should tell you how to correct any errors found but one or two basic principles are worth mentioning here.

a) The measured distance needs to be of a reasonable length and must be easy to see. Ideally there would be a transit at either end of the distance so that an absolutely accurate distance can be sailed.

b) The water along the measured distance should be calm if possible or at least consistent. Wash from other vessels can produce significant errors.

c) It must be possible to sail on the correct course for the full distance without having to alter course for other vessels. Measured miles within a shipping channel are not particularly suited for this reason, unless it is possible to proceed just outside the channel.

d) If doing the calibration in an area with any current or tidal stream it is always worth doing three runs, then using twice the middle values to average against the first and third runs. This means that if the current is changing any changes should be cancelled out. It will also be better to perform the runs when the tide is at its maximum or at least not at the turn of the tide in order to minimize difference between runs.

Wind speed

The anemometer should have been factory calibrated and is unlikely to be in error. However, it is possible that there will be

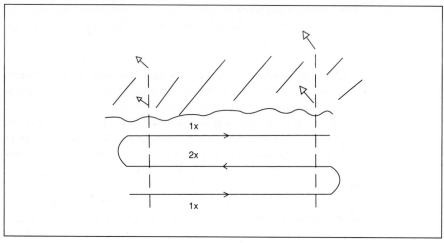

54 Three runs for distance/speed calibration

differences in wind speed on various points of sail due to the closeness of the masthead to the anemometer and also at differing angles of heel. The better systems will use an algorithm to correct for the angle of heel, but only if the yacht also has a heel indicator within the instrument system.

The position of the cups in relation to the masthead are normally best dealt with on an empirical basis, noting the wind speed when head to wind on a day with reasonably steady winds, and then turning the yacht around and noting wind speeds at all other angles. The presence of the masthead will usually produce an increase in wind speed of one-three knots when going downwind because of the localized acceleration of the wind over the mast. Any increase which is noted can then be removed either manually from any calculations or, if possible, by including the values as internal corrections within the system software (such as within the B&G 690 system).

55 Acceleration of wind over the masthead

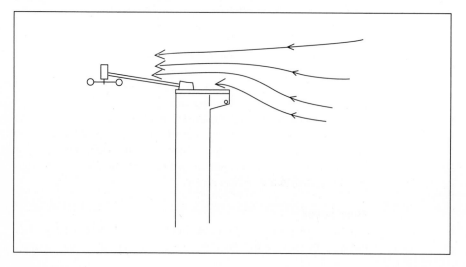

Wind vane alignment

Checking that the wind angle is zero when head to wind is one of the first calibration tasks which needs to be carried out. It is usually most accurate to do this with someone at the masthead while in the harbour. Get them to align the vane with a straight edge along the centre line of the yacht and note what the apparent wind angle is reading.

Depending on the sophistication of the system, it may be possible to correct for any small misalignment through the software or it may be necessary to realign the mounting bracket physically.

Wind shear

One problem which will occur from time to time is that of wind shear. Unless there is good mixing of air from different levels (normally by convection on a sunny day), the wind at sea level will be slowed down by the surface friction and will normally be backed compared to the wind aloft due to the direction of the spin of the earth (the reverse is true in the southern hemisphere).

This may not seem to be a very significant problem, but it can be. On a dull day with stratus clouds and little or no mixing of the air, it is common to see shear from deck level to the masthead of as much as 20° and in exceptional circumstances there may be much more than this.

56 Wind shear

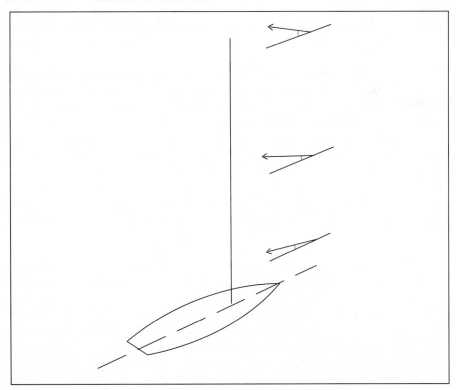

The effect of this on your sailing is to make the masthead alignment appear to be all wrong since on one tack you would be sailing with a wind angle of, say, 50° while on the other the wind angle may only be 20°. Unless understood, this can quickly lead to the outputs from the instruments not being relied upon since the shear is usually diagnosed as an instrument fault.

Unless you have a very simple and quick method of changing the masthead alignment it is usually best to live with the effect of shear but to be aware of the implications on other displays. For example VMG and any associated functions will be wrong.

The problem with shear is keeping track of how much shear there is at any given moment. In sea breeze-type conditions, with light offshore winds early on, there is likely to be considerable shear until the sea breeze comes in when it will suddenly disappear. If a correction has been applied, it then needs to be removed or reduced whenever necessary.

If you suspect that there is a significant amount of shear on a particular day, it is wise to inform the trimmers so that they can adjust their sheet leads accordingly and also to let the helmsman know because the numbers on one tack will be much better than those on the other tack.

Magnetic wind direction

Before the magnetic wind direction can possibly be correct, the basic inputs need to be calibrated (boat speed, compass heading and wind speed).

The final correction will be to the true wind angle, since this will also affect the magnetic wind direction. Not many systems will allow correction or calibration at this level but the top racing installations should. The true wind angle is going to be significantly affected by upwash from the sails and this is a very difficult error to allow for in calibrations. Some manufacturers will attempt to use an algorithm for this correction, but this has never been a very successful route.

In my experience the best way to correct for upwash and all other associated errors is empirically, looking at correction factors which actually work on your yacht in a certain set of conditions. The B&G 690 instruments allow this in a very neat and manageable way. There is a user-accessible look-up table of corrections for beating, running and reaching for every 5 knots of wind speed. In a particular wind speed, first look at the magnetic wind direction through a tack. If it appears to tack with you (that is move right as you turn right), then the true wind angle is too small and vice versa if the magnetic wind direction appears to change in the opposite way to that of the tack.

For example, if the magnetic wind direction on starboard tack is indicating, say, 235° but then changes to indicate 245° when on port tack, then this shows an error of 10°. In this case a correction of plus five degrees needs to be applied to the true wind angle, (+) because the wind changed in the same direction as the turn and (five degrees) because only half the error needs to be applied as a correction because it will be applied on both tacks.

57 Corrections to true wind angle for Mag, wind direction

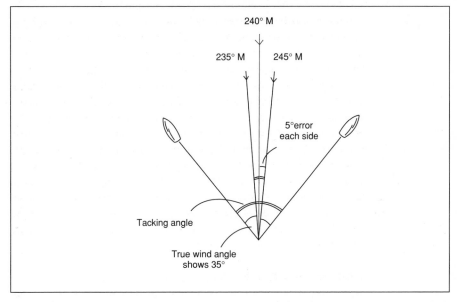

Having got the magnetic wind direction to stay constant when tacking, it is then just necessary to bear away from close hauled to a beam reach and apply corrections in the same way. Then finally go from close hauled to a run and apply those corrections.

**7.6
COMPUTERS
AFLOAT**

It could be said with some justification that any of the instruments which I have been describing earlier in this chapter contain computers, but in this section I am talking about portable computers which, while being integrated into the instrument systems, do much more than simply link some instruments together.

For a computer to be of real value inshore or on small racing yachts, it must be waterproof and rugged enough to stand up to use in the cockpit. It must also be understood by the crew on the yacht and must produce figures or information which is of real value in itself. If all these criteria are not met, there is a real danger that time, money and effort will be wasted on trying to use a computer simply because the Admiral's Cup and America's Cup boats use them.

I have used several different computers with success, all of which are relatively complex and expensive beasts. This makes it unlikely that they will be seen on any low-budget campaigns. Most, with the exception of MacSea, attempted to do roughly the same job and all need to be linked into both the yacht's instruments and the position fixer. In essence, they merely extend the capabilities of a system such as the B&G 690, but this extension opens up possibilities for the navigator which are too difficult to imagine unless you have seen the systems in use.

The three tactical systems I have dealt with are called Deckman, Tacstar and TIAC (Tactics in a Chip). Deckman was the first system to become fully developed and was originally produced for the America's Cup circus. With the Mark I version costing around £6,000, they were only seen on yachts with large budgets, but as with most electronics, and computers in particular, prices have tumbled at about the same rate as features have increased and the latest Deckman is available for under £2,000 as a full system complete with rugged waterproof computer, software and connectors. This brings it down to about the same cost as a new sail (or possibly two new sails) and it is now a real option in top club racing yachts.

Having used it more than any other type of navigation computer, I am a fan of Deckman which seems to do just about everything that I want to ask of it. Even in its Mark II guise, however, it is not a simple piece of software to get the best results from. Each system has merits and problems and owners/navigators should look at what is currently available before buying a particular piece of equipment.

Before even thinking about an integrated computer system, the yacht must have instruments which can be connected to it. This can either be through the NMEA-type interface or through an RS232 interface. The former is much more common but generally only allows communication one way - from the instruments to the computer whereas the RS232 allows the computer to talk to the instruments as well as receiving data from them. The advantage of being able to talk to the instruments is that computer-corrected or generated data such as target speeds, accurate true wind figures and so on can then be displayed for all the crew to see. If using a one-way system, only the navigator can see the correct data and the rest of the crew have to put up with uncorrected figures, which can obviously cause confusion.

The sorts of things which this type of system can do are as follows:

a) Graphic display of averages: wind speed, wind direction, VMG, etc.

b) Plot of current position on a simple chart of the course, together with laylines, times to layline, etc.

c) Course to steer allowing for the internally held tidal streams.

d) Correction of instruments through a set of look-up tables.

e) Ability to look at other legs of the course with either the present or manually input values for wind and tide.

f) Full speed polar tables with various methods for updating the data.

g) Time and distance to the start line (with Deckman, if linked to GPS).

h) Simple routeing facility (with Deckman). Taking predicted wind and tide into account, Deckman will effectively go through a series of 'what if?' scenarios in a way that is impossible without a computer.

This list is not exhaustive by any means. Both these and other similar computers are having their software continually modified and improved and the list of functions and capabilities expands all the time.

In order to get the best out of a computer of this type, it is important that all the basics of racing navigation are understood beforehand. It would be wrong to think that a computer will answer all the questions for you - it may well be capable of doing this but only if you know which questions to ask!

One computer system that has taken a rather different line in its development to those described above is the Apple-based MacSea. This was produced, in its early stages at least, for long distance, transocean racers and concentrates on routeing and associated functions. It now gives a lot of the same form of tactical data as do the others and should be considered as an option, particularly on larger yachts or for those who enter longer races.

8   Electronic Navaids

In the distant past when I first started to navigate real racing yachts offshore, the nearest thing to an electronic navaid was a radio direction finder. Since even automatic versions of these were banned until the early 1980s, we poor navigators had to make do with pointing a radio with a ferrite rod aerial attached towards the nearest marine radio beacon in order to get a bearing from the null signal. As can be imagined, this was never a very accurate system but at least it was (and is) capable of giving bearings to within about five degrees when inside the range of the appropriate beacon.

Ever since the Second World War, Decca has been available as a fixing system in Northern Europe, but until quite recently it was only allowed to be used in rented sets with Decca taking a large rental each year. This was fine on commercial ships and fishing boats but was never really developed in a suitable format for yachts until the mid 1980s. Also, it was banned for most racing at least in the UK since it was perceived to be too big an advantage which money alone could obtain. In other parts of the world, especially North America, the Loran system flourished and indeed was (and is) widely used by yachts whether cruising or racing. A system of satellite navigation was also developed which used a doppler shift caused by fairly low and fast satellites passing overhead to give fixes. This was ideal for cruising but not so good for inshore racing since the satellites only passed overhead about once every 90 minutes or so.

Early in the 1980s there was a major change in racing policy, led by the Royal Ocean Racing Club and the bans on such things as automatic fixing devices, linked instrument systems and the like were abolished - to the inevitable cries of 'shame' from traditionalists! This quickly led to better and better systems with boxes coming down in price, size and battery consumption until at last there were good, relatively cheap and reliable fixing systems available for more or less all yachts. There was a short period of stabilization when the Decca and Loran were the best available, giving fixes accurate to within a few hundred metres, most of the time. The traditionalists found that it was still necessary to navigate by more old-fashioned means in order to keep a check on the electronics and more importantly that this modern wizardry did not destroy the sport of offshore racing and actually enhanced most aspects of it.

Then in 1990 came the next era of accuracy in position fixing with the advent of the Global Positioning System (GPS) of satellites. These provide all-weather 24-hour fixes anywhere in the world to within a few tens of metres and allow hitherto undreamed of functions to become practicable. It is still necessary to keep a track on where you are by reference to a chart for when the electrics do give problems, as they inevitably do usually when you can least cope with the hassle of losing your electronic position.

General Principles

**8.1
NAVAIDS –
GLOBAL
POSITIONING
SYSTEM (GPS)**

GPS is the latest positioning system to have been introduced and as such it is more accurate and (hopefully) more reliable than any of its predecessors. Once the whole system is installed it should provide 24-hour worldwide coverage with no interference from the weather.

The system consists of a constellation of 24 satellites, orbiting at the extremely high altitude of 10,900 miles. The plan is to have 21 active satellites with three spares in orbit so that the system should not collapse if or when a satellite ceases to function. With this number of satellites orbiting that high, it should be possible to 'see' at least four of them at any time, thus making three-dimensional fixes a reality for aircraft (and missiles). For yachtsmen, having four satellites in view should give excellent two-dimensional fixes with the fourth satellite giving a check on the position.

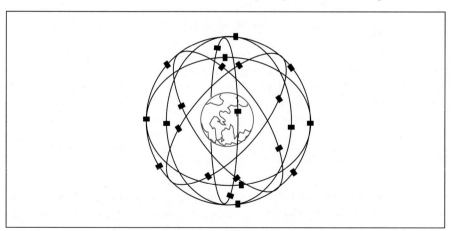

58 GPS satellite array

The principle on which GPS works is the accurate measurement of distance from the receiver (actually the antenna) to a number of satellites. Each satellite transmits an extremely precise time signal as well as data to give its position. In essence it is simply a ranging system using accurate knowledge of the position of each satellite. The range from each satellite gives one position line (a sphere of position around the satellite) and it takes three such position lines to give a two-dimensional fix.

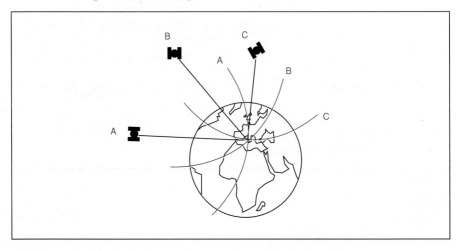

Accuracy

Originally designed for the United States military, there are two levels of accuracy within the same system. The most accurate for military and specific licensed civilian users is called the Precise Positioning Service (PPS) and this will give fixes to better than 10m. Ordinary civilian users, including all yachtsmen, will not be able to use the PPS due to the inclusion of specially encrypted signals from the satellites. They (we) have access to a slightly less accurate Standard Positioning Service which should still be accurate to better than 20m at most times. Additionally, some of the satellites known collectively as 'block ll' have the potential to degrade their signal further in a selective way. This can limit accuracy to about 100m, still perfectly adequate for most purposes, but not for rock hopping.

As well as the above inaccuracies, the actual geometry of the satellites being used can affect the accuracy to quite a large degree. Since the range from each satellite will have a certain amount of error (a few metres), this will translate into an area of uncertainty when the three position lines are put together, in much the same way as one gets a cocked hat with a simple three-bearing fix. The nearer the satellites are together in an angular plane, the greater will be the error. This is shown in diagram 60. The errors are shown as the actual ranging errors multiplied by a factor called the Horizontal Dilution of Precision (HDOP). A small HDOP means that the satellites are well placed in relation to one another whereas a large HDOP means that the fix may not be so accurate. As a guide, HDOP figures of less than 4.5 will give acceptable fixes.

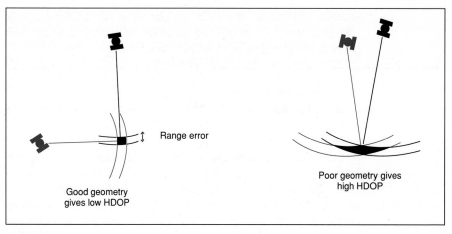

60 Satellite
geometry
relates to HDOP

General Principles

**8.2
NAVAIDS –
DECCA AND
LORAN**

61 Decca or
Loran - hyperbolic
position lines

Decca and Loran are both ground-based radio systems which, although using totally different principles for their internal working, look very much the same to the user. Both have chains of stations, with a master and two or three slave stations in each chain and both give hyperbolic lines of position. Decca was developed in the UK during the Second World War while Loran was developed in the USA.

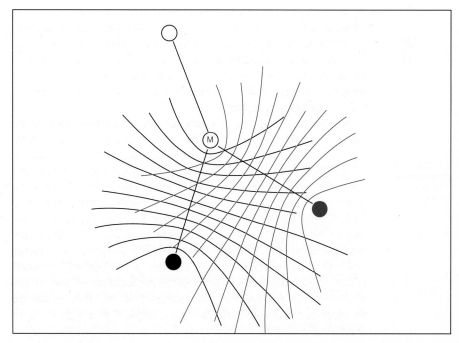

Decca utilizes a measurement of the phase difference between signals from the master station and each slave to give its position lines, whereas Loran uses a measurement of the time difference between the signals for its position lines. For the user these differences between the two systems are of chiefly academic interest although, as can be seen under the heading of 'errors', the use of phase differences can give Decca users more of a headache than that experienced by users of the Loran chains.

For both systems it is possible to buy charts with the appropriate lattice of position lines over-printed onto them with this being the most accurate way to utilize the systems since fixed errors can then be accommodated. For most yachtsmen, this use of lattice charts is too much of a nuisance and sets have been developed which convert the raw position lines into latitude- and longitude-type positions.

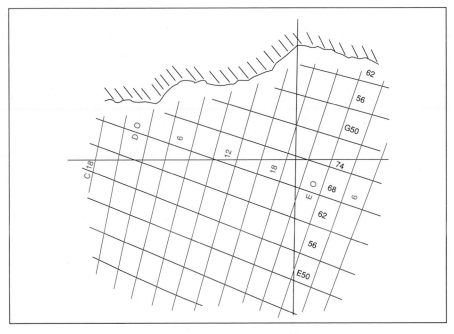

62 Extract from a lattice chart (Decca or Loran)

Although both Decca and Loran have served the mariner well over a number of years, the advent of GPS has spelled the eventual death knell of both systems due to their less accurate fixes and lack of worldwide coverage.

Errors associated with Decca and Loran

a) Fixed errors: Both systems are prone to certain geographically fixed errors due to the refraction of radio waves around some coastlines. Typically, these errors can give positional differences of up to about 1/4 mile. The repeatability of positions is much better than this with accuracies of around 50-100m being normal.

This difference between absolute accuracy and the repeatability of a fix means that if using a system for going to the same waypoint more than once, the actual Decca or Loran position of the waypoint should be noted because then the next time you go to the same waypoint your set will give a much more accurate position. Furthermore, if an error of say $^1/4$ mile is found at one waypoint, it is a reasonably safe assumption that there will be a similar error for a limited distance around that waypoint as well and this can be applied to other fixes when comparing the electronic position with actual positions marked on the chart.

b) Base-line extension: All navigators will be familiar with the concept that if using bearings to take a fix, the wider apart the objects are, the more accurate will be the fix. Also, if the objects are very close together (say within about five degrees), although this gives you a good position line in one direction, any error in angle will produce a large error along that position line.

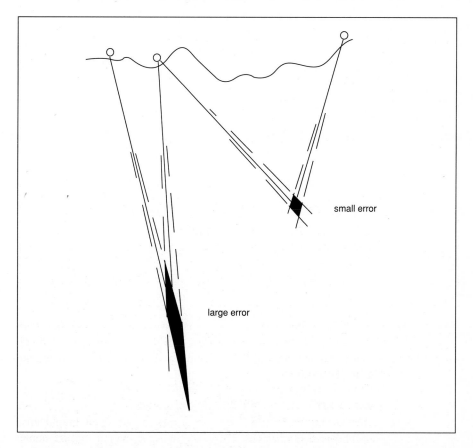

small error

large error

63 Poor angle of cut gives potentially larger error

The same is true with positions obtained from hyperbolical position lines such as those given by Decca or Loran. If you are either on or near the extension of the line drawn through the master to a slave, this gives you exactly the same effect as having a narrow angle of cut between bearings and so large errors towards or away from the stations can be expected.

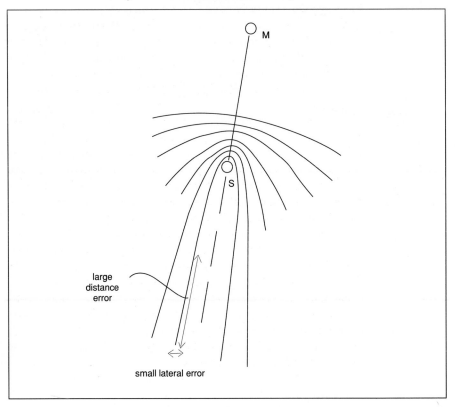

64 Baseline extension - Decca

I have seen a Decca set give errors of this nature of up to five miles while the Decca set was quite happily giving a 'green' fix. Obviously, the accuracy at right angles to the position lines is very good.

The solution to this problem is twofold. First, the prudent navigator should be aware of the problem and should know when it may become significant to his own navigation. Secondly, if base-line extension errors are occurring, changing manually to another chain will nearly always solve the problem even if this decreases the theoretical accuracy a little because of the extra distance from the chain.

c) Dawn and dusk errors: It is a well-known fact that certain radio waves are reflected by the ionosphere more at dawn and dusk than at any other time and this is certainly true of both Decca and Loran transmissions. This sometimes has the effect of confusing the receiver into thinking that the sky wave is in fact the ground wave and because the sky wave will have travelled a longer distance to reach the receiver, this can give quite large errors.

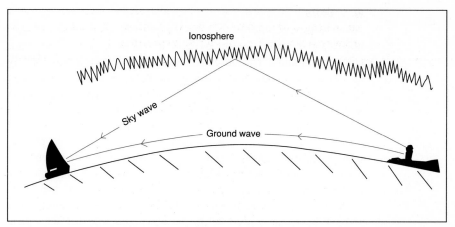

Ionosphere

Sky wave

Ground wave

65 Dawn/dusk effect - sky waves

d) Jumping lanes: Because Decca uses a measurement of phase difference to determine how far you are away from the master and slave transmitters, and because almost by definition the wave pattern is repeated at regular intervals, it is quite possible for a Decca set to become confused as to which wave it is in even though it will know exactly where it is in relationship to the wave itself. The wave patterns which provide the position lines will repeat themselves about every four-eight miles (depending on your distance from the transmitters), thus it is always important to know your position to better than this when using Decca just in case it thinks you are one or two waves away from your actual position.

e) Use of the sky wave: Once again because Decca uses phase differences it is not possible to make use of the signals which have reflected from the ionosphere to give a fix. With Loran, it is possible to use these signals, as long as the receiver 'knows' that it is receiving a sky wave and is not mixing sky wave signals and ground wave signals together. This gives Loran a much greater useful range than Decca has, albeit with significantly reduced accuracy.

Position

8.3
NAVAIDS -
USEFUL
FUNCTIONS

All of the navaids, whether it be Decca, Loran or GPS has position fixing as its base function and therefore the current position of the yacht should always be available as a display. In most systems, this position will be given as latitude and longitude, with most Decca and Loran giving the position to hundredths of a mile while GPS sets give the position to the nearest thousandth.

One point which is always worth bearing in mind is that although the sets give readings to these extreme accuracies, it does not mean that the actual positions are necessarily this accurate! One thousandth of a mile is after all only two yards and even GPS on a good day is not that precise.

Waypoints

All sets should be able to have the position of a buoy or other object input manually and used as a reference point. These are called waypoints. The normal method of inputting a waypoint is by latitude and longitude and most modern sets allow the storage of dozens or even hundreds of such positions, sometimes in groups so that each area can have its own set of waypoints.

It is possible with some sets to input the position of a waypoint by giving range and bearing information, either from the present position of the yacht or from another waypoint. If this function is allowed, it should be used with extreme caution since small angular errors can produce large inaccuracies in position over a distance.

As well as having the waypoints input into the receiver, I like to have hard, paper copy of all the waypoints together with their number in the bank and their positions. This can be extremely useful as reference or of course if another receiver is ever used, for example on another yacht.

Bearing and distance

One of the most used functions will be a simple bearing and distance to a selected waypoint from the bank. This can be used as an alternative to latitude and longitude for plotting the position of the yacht as well as giving a simple idea of how far it is to the next mark.

If the centre of a compass rose on the chart is used as a waypoint it is extremely easy to plot from that. For example, if, as in diagram 66, the navaid says that you are in a position 3.2 miles from the compass rose and your bearing to it is 150°(m), all you need to do is draw a line along the reciprocal of 150° and measure off 3.2 miles to give your actual position. This is often simpler than going to the latitude and longitude scales and plotting position using them.

66 Using compass rose as 'centre' waypoint

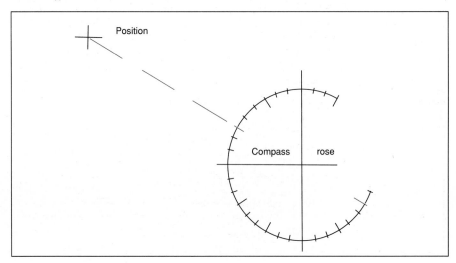

Beware with bearing and distance, however, do not forget that if you were 60 miles from a waypoint you would need to move one mile sideways before the bearing changed by one degree. To put this into perspective, if approaching a buoy from, say, 10 miles out, each degree of bearing is equivalent to about 300m difference in position. This means that if attempting to sail down a bearing line to arrive at the buoy, this method would not tell you that your course was in error until you had moved 300m from the rhumb line.

Cross-track error

Cross-track error simply means the distance your yacht has moved from a fixed line, normally the rhumb line between waypoints. On Decca and Loran sets it will usually be given in hundredths of a mile (as for position), thus it will alter each time the yacht moves a further 20m from the rhumb line. With GPS sets cross-track error will often be given to the nearest thousandth of a mile and will thus be even more precise.

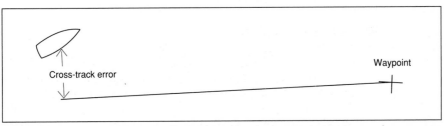

67 Cross-track error

There are at least three ways that cross-track error can be used. The first, which is the way that most cruising navigators would use, is to leave cross-track error building up from one waypoint until the next waypoint is reached. This allows the navigator to monitor easily how far the tidal streams have swept the yacht (in total) and to see whether the original assumptions on course to steer and so on are being borne out in reality.

I use cross-track error in a second way and that is to reset it to zero each time I plot a fix. In this way it is possible to see how the course steered is working out over shorter periods of time. It also means that the rhumb line being used is the more relevant one of your position to the next mark, rather than mark to mark which becomes purely hypothetical.

68 Reset cross-track error at each fix

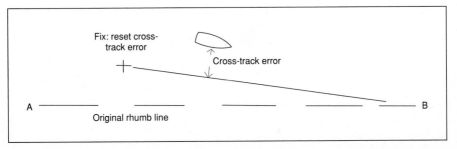

Another time that cross-track error can be useful is in giving you a safe line in the same way as a clearing bearing is used. Set up a waypoint either side of the danger and monitor your position relative to this as you go past the danger.

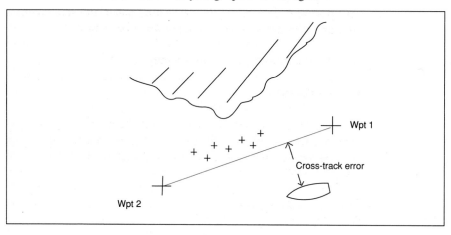

69 Cross-track error for clearing line

Route or sail plan

In order to use the waypoints in most receivers it is necessary to set up a route (or sail plan) consisting of a number of waypoints in the order of rounding. Typically this would be the course with each mark or turning point as a separate waypoint within the sequence.

One problem that can occur while using a sail plan with some receivers is that if you merely pass the buoy rather than rounding it the set may not automatically flick over to the next waypoint. This is because in most cases it is necessary to pass close to the

70 Waypoint may not be set properly

buoy in order to get it to switch and at the same time to go past the angle bisector between the waypoints as shown in diagram 70.

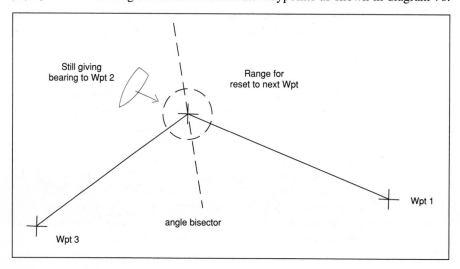

Centre function

This is a waypoint function where only one waypoint is in use rather than relating to a route or sail plan. It can be very useful especially around the start line where one end of the line can be set up as the centre point. It can also be handy to use a compass rose as a centre point for reference when on long races.

Course and speed (over the ground)

Because the position fixer gives a fairly accurate position more or less continuously, it is possible to get a readout of the average course and speed over the ground over a preset period.

With Decca and Loran, using a time of about five minutes is probably the fastest average which will give realistic course and speed figures. This is because, with repeatability accuracies of around 50-100m and normal boat speeds, shorter time scales just give less and less accurate courses and speeds as the jumps in position become more and more significant. The faster the boat speed the better and, indeed, at very slow ground speeds it may be impossible to get any useful data from this function.

The increased accuracy of the GPS system allows far better use of course and speed information. It is common to be able to get consistent readings with a time period as low as one minute and in some cases even as low as 30 seconds. This means that it is feasible to use the data as a source of real-time tidal stream information, when the GPS system is linked into the yacht's instruments. From a navigator's point of view this is an enormous step forward and allows accurate assessments of, for example, when a counter current is being experienced or whether it is better to be on one side of a bank or the other.

Even with the greater accuracy derived from the GPS system, this function is probably best not used to gauge your real ground track - unless a long average is being used - and cross-track error will give a better idea of whether a particular track is being maintained.

Accuracy and error functions

All good sets will give various options to look at such things as signal-to-noise ratio, HDOP, Decca chain data, etc. Most will also give error signals when something is not quite right. These should be obvious but also easily switched off. It is very annoying to have a GPS receiver start bleeping at the five-minute gun and have to go into a complicated procedure to switch off the bleep.

Especially with GPS, whose accuracy can be so good as to show up the limitations of charting, it is important to have the facility to enter different chart datums for use with charts from the various charting authorities around the world.

Magnetic variation

Some people always work on a chart in true degrees, others always work in magnetic while some, such as myself, work in whatever is most convenient at the time. When using range and bearing or any other function which gives a bearing or course, it is obviously vital that it is known which system the navaid is displaying.

I like to have all information of this type displayed in magnetic notation and therefore have to remember to input the local variation whenever the receiver is reset.

Man-overboard function

This is often a well-advertised function in the promotion for a navaid but in my opinion it has very limited use and can even be dangerous, especially if sailing in an area of strong or unknown current.

The principle is that when a help button is pressed, the set will memorize the current position at that time and give a continuous range and bearing back to that position. The idea being that if you get the range to zero then you should be next to the man in the water. The problem is of course that you will actually return to the same geographical position but in the meantime the man may have drifted a considerable distance down tide.

My view is that this can be a useful absolute last-ditch function for use when you have lost sight of the man and cannot find him by other means. If you pressed the panic button as he fell in the water, this at least gives you a starting position from which to search.

Estimated time of arrival

I think this function has limited use on a racing yacht. It relies for accuracy on the yacht maintaining a constant speed and the tidal stream also staying constant.

Miscellaneous functions

Most sets have various other secondary functions such as battery voltage, anchor function (a variation of the centre point function), etc. within their repertoires, some of which can be genuinely useful. It is worth reading the handbook for your particular set to ascertain just which functions are available.

**8.4
CHOICE
OF RECEIVER**

A book of this nature cannot hope to be able to give up-to-date information on which set to purchase since any information would be out of date before the book was even published. There are, however, certain general guidelines which will remain valid for the foreseeable future.

GPS, Decca or Loran?

If you already have a Decca or Loran receiver then it is well worth keeping that as a back up to GPS, but if going out to purchase a new set I would recommend buying GPS as the first navaid - assuming that the budget allows.

Things to look for

a) Reliability: Ultimately this is more important than almost anything else. Complex functions and good compatibility with your instruments are of no use whatsoever if the receiver is not working.

b) Compatibility: If it may be necessary to connect the navaid into the other yacht instrument systems, it is very important to ensure that the systems are mutually compatible. This includes the appropriate NMEA or RS232 interface if required.

c) Functions: Do not worry unduly about looking for the receiver with the most functions unless they are really going to be of use. Sometimes, a simple set with enough of the basic functions will be easier to use and therefore ultimately of more use than a very sophisticated but complex set.

d) Multi-channel receiver: I would always want a multi-channel receiver since this allows all satellites to be tracked at the same time and therefore provides real simultaneous fixes. A single-channel receiver must first lock onto and then fix from each satellite in turn - this may well take less than a minute but it will still degrade the accuracy of the ultimate fix, and thus all related functions (such as course and speed) will also be degraded.

As an emergency set or one used just for cruising, the cost savings inherent in single-channel receivers may make them worth considering, but not for a racing yacht.

e) Voltage range: The receiver should be as tolerant as possible of voltage changes. If this is not the case it is likely that the thing will reset itself every time the engine is turned on or off (unless there is a totally separate starting battery) or if the voltage drops for any other reason.

f) Waterproof?: Unless the set is going to be linked into the main instrument system it is worth considering the best place for it before purchase. There are only a few sets which can be safely installed in an open cockpit and this may decide the choice. Alternatively, some sets offer cockpit repeaters for at least some of their functions.

**8.5
SENSIBLE
BACKUP**

Modern electronics are becoming incredibly reliable. There was a time not many years ago when you would consider yourself pretty lucky if all the instruments kept going for a whole race. The situation has now largely reversed itself and one would feel fairly unlucky to have a major breakdown of electronics during the course of an average season. That is of course as long as they are all installed properly in the first place and high-quality equipment is used.

Having extolled the virtues of modern electronics, it still does not change the fact that however accurate an electronic navaid may be and however reliable it is (usually), there will inevitably come a time when something does go wrong and for this reason it is really important to maintain the capability of continuing by the use of traditional navigation techniques.

My view is that the minimum navigation required in addition to just looking at the GPS or Decca is to record the position regularly while the receiver is working. I like to keep a simple logbook going at least on offshore races and record the latitude and longitude at least once an hour and normally more often than that. This means that if the set should suddenly stop working for any reason, you only have a maximum of one hour of plotting before getting up to date. For this to work effectively, you must also record approximate speeds and courses or distances run from each course change.

71 Simple
logbook entries

| Time | DR | | Position | | Remarks |
	Hdg	Dist	Lat	Long	
0335	Reset		–	–	EC2 abeam
0400	010	2.1	50 degrees 14.2	1 degree 12.4	GPS
0440	005	3.3	50 degrees 17.5	1 degree 11.6	tacked to port
0500	Reset 035	5.8	50 degrees 18.1	1 degree 08.9	GPS - plotted

When using a GPS receiver this is probably all that is required. However, when using Decca, which can have quite large errors if on a baseline extension or if one slave station goes out of action, it is also worth keeping a rough idea of the estimated position between fixes and comparing the E.P. with the Decca fix each time a fix is plotted.

72 Compare
Decca to EP

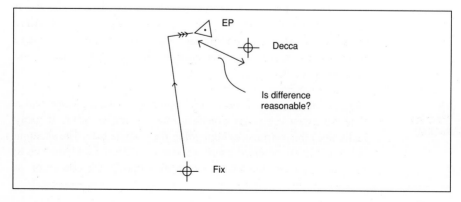

Yeoman plotter

The Navigator's Yeoman is a development from the computer industry which uses ordinary charts and speeds up all aspects of plotting or extracting bearings and positions.

The system comprises a Plotting Board with the Yeoman computer attached to it and connected by a spiral cable to a unit called the 'Puck'. This consists of a liquid crystal display and seven function keys. The chart is clipped to the plotting board and referenced to it so that the computer can sense the position of the puck on the chart. It is possible (although not essential) to link the Yeoman into the position-fixing device when it uses a standard NMEA interface. When this has been done, the Yeoman allows easy and quick plotting of the current position as well as bearings to and from any other position on the chart.

I was sceptical about its usefulness until presented with one on board *Wings of Oracle* for the 1991 Admiral's Cup. Here I found that for offshore races it saved a lot of time and really sped up plotting positions no end. This was especially true in light airs when it was feasible to navigate much of the time from below decks. When one considers that on *Wings of Oracle* I was really spoilt for equipment and had a fully operational Deckman computer as well, it is no small testimony to the Yeoman that it was still a valuable piece of equipment.

73 Yeoman plotter
- uses ordinary
charts

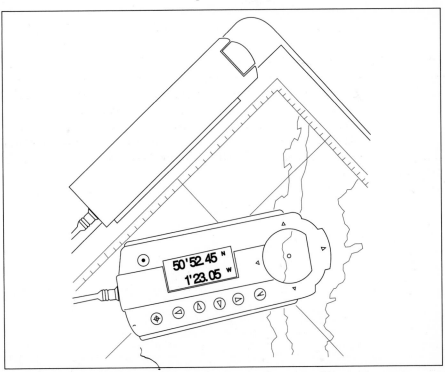

Electronic charts

It is now possible to get digitized versions of most charts around the world and this has made it possible to manufacture electronic charts. Essentially these have a display screen on which is shown the required part of the chart. Most have controls for zooming in or out of a particular section and when integrated with the position fixer they will display the current position of the yacht.

Although they take the convenience of the Yeoman plotter one stage further still, I have never found them to be as useful on a racing yacht. My main complaint, if that is the correct word, is that it is not easy to update the charts and new versions need to be obtained as and when they are available. This inevitably means that the charts themselves are not as up to date as a properly corrected paper chart would be, and thus there is always an element of doubt as to the accuracy of the information.

There will come the time, however, when the facilities available with Deckman or Tacstar computers will be merged with electronic charts to give the all-in-one navigation and performance system. This is something to look forward to.

9   Overall Strategy

Strategy is the overall navigational game plan in the absence of the rest of the fleet. The interaction with other yachts will be dealt with later in the chapter on tactics. In real situations it is very often difficult to separate the two subjects completely since one will nearly always be influenced by the other, but for our purposes here it is convenient to consider them apart.

This chapter will look at the overall game plan and will follow a logical sequence around a hypothetical race course. Hence we shall begin with the start, then cover beating legs, then the windward mark and so on until the finish. In most situations it does not really matter whether you are dealing with an inshore or an offshore race, although in the former case tactics will often need more emphasis placed on them than strategy and vice versa offshore.

**9.1
TIDAL
STRATEGY**

There are some tidal questions which are best looked at on a leg-by-leg basis and others which cross these boundaries and which are therefore best dealt with in a more general way. This section endeavours to look at some of the latter.

In an ideal world you would always be in the maximum tide whenever it was with you and would get into the areas with the least tide when it was against you. In practice this is obviously not always possible, but it should normally be at the back of your mind as something to strive towards. In order to be able to achieve the best possible position it is vital that you not only have the best tidal information available but also understand how to interpret that information.

If you are sailing along a coast which has bays and headlands, then it is likely that the strongest current will be at or near the headlands with a corresponding reduction in current as you go into the bays. There is normally also a sweep out of a bay as you approach a headland if the stream is with you, but the set into the bay when the stream is against you is nearly always significantly less pronounced (see diagram 74).

Once you have got inside the direct line from headland to headland, the tidal gradient as you go deeper into a bay is not often great until you get very close to the shore. This means that when sailing against the stream it is rarely worth diving right into bays in an attempt to get out of the stream unless you can do so without increasing the distance sailed, for example when beating.

Another major factor in deciding how far to go into a bay is the size and time scale involved. If you go hard into this particular bay to get out of a foul stream, will this put you in a less advantageous position when the tide turns? You must always be looking at the overall plan and not get bogged down in short-term detail.

74 Current in a typical bay

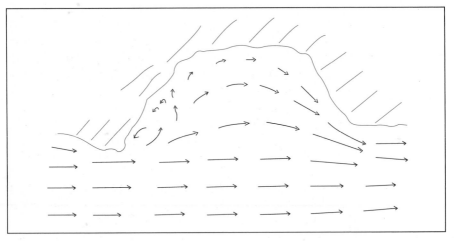

9.2 WIND STRATEGY

The utilization of wind shifts will vary from leg to leg but one aspect of forecasting applies regardless of which leg you are on at the time - the amount of wind. There is no point going the 'right way' for a wind shift if by so doing you experience significantly less wind.

This was exemplified beautifully during the 1991 Fastnet Race when *Wings of Oracle*, which I was navigating, sailed around the fleet on the outside of a 40° wind bend to end up 11 miles ahead of the next Two-Tonner by the Fastnet rock. We did this by keeping in better pressure to the west of the remainder of our fleet while they were virtually becalmed. If we had merely applied traditional theory to a situation like that without thinking the situation right through, we would have gone the other way and lost out heavily.

The lesson to be learnt there is that wind pressure is just as important as wind direction, especially in light airs. It is often worth going in almost the completely wrong direction, as long as you are still moving and as long as you are getting closer to your destination. In order to be able to do that you must have good forecasting on your boat, either actual single observer forecasting (looking at the current situation and interpreting it yourself), or at least good access to and understanding of the available weather forecasts.

It is possible in certain circumstances to find significantly different wind strengths as well as different wind directions within quite small geographical areas. We have all seen on an inshore race how maybe one side or the other will pay - just because of more pressure or because of a persistent geographical shift. As was shown in the 1991 Fastnet, this also happens offshore, albeit often for different reasons and you must be on the look out for 'better wind'.

Whichever leg you are on it is well worth monitoring the positions of your competitors to see if they are doing better or worse than expected. You can often pick up the fact that one side of the course is being favoured in time to get across to the favoured side and before everyone else has gone! I favour a plotting sheet, drawn out more or less to scale, on which to plot the positions of the fleet. Relative positions can normally be estimated with a hand-bearing compass and a guess of distance, although a range finder does help and especially in light airs the use of a sextant for vertical angles on the masts of your competitors is not such a daft idea.

Do not forget that the strength and direction of the current will affect the sailing wind (see tidal wind in chapter 3). This means that if you can get out of a foul current by sailing, for example, the other side of a sand bank, or you can get into more favourable current in another situation, this will also affect your sailing wind and if wind and tide are in opposition this may give you a proportionally bigger gain than you anticipated. However, if the wind and current are together, the drop in wind speed may nullify the tidal gain. Also, if you are sailing during the change in the tide, this will affect the sailing wind and will probably give you a totally predictable wind shift (and possibly change in wind strength).

9.3
THE START

The start can count for much more than just the few seconds gained or lost in actually crossing the line, particularly in an inshore race. Having the advantage of clear air up the first leg by getting a good start obviously pays handsome dividends, whereas trying to recover from a bad start often leads to your following a second-rate strategy in order to try to get clear air. Although in an offshore race there is more time to recover from this bad start, the first beat is normally longer and therefore you are likely to be suffering in dirt for a long time, so do not underestimate the importance of getting a good start even in long races.

Upwind starts

Whenever possible a good race committee will endeavour to give you an upwind start because this should give the fairest start to the whole fleet and will allow the fleet to spread out before they get to the first mark.

Bias relative to the wind

As far as strategy is concerned an upwind start is normally fairly straightforward. The first consideration is the angle of the line relative to the wind direction. As long as you have to tack in order to reach the first mark, the actual position of the mark can be ignored but the 'bias' of the line is critical.

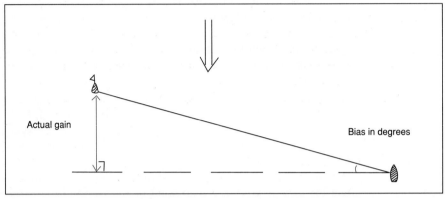

Actual gain

Bias in degrees

75 Start line - bias

As can be seen from the diagram 75, the advantage given by bias is substantial. Even on a reasonably short line of say 400m, each five degrees of bias gives a distance advantage of about 35m and on longer lines the advantage obviously becomes even greater. There are two different ways to determine the bias of the line. The first method, more suitable to dinghies than yachts although it can be used by boats of any size, is to sail along the line in one direction with just the mainsail up and to sheet the main until it is correctly set. Then tack around and sail along the line the opposite way, once again trimming the sail correctly. The favoured end will be the one you are pointing towards with the sail sheeted in harder - because this will automatically be the end which is furthest upwind.

76 Checking for bias

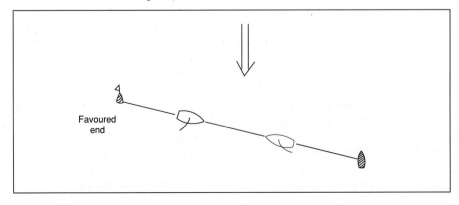

Favoured end

The problems with the above simple method of determining the favoured end of the line are that it does not tell you how much bias there is, you must be able to sail actually along the line, if the wind changes direction you will have to start again. There is therefore a better way of measuring the bias which gets over all these problems. If you first measure the actual bearing of the line, either with a hand-bearing compass or by sailing along the line and noting the compass heading, you can then compare that bearing with the wind direction and calculate which end is favoured. Thus, if the line is bearing, say, 260° and you are starting to the north, then a wind of 260° + 90° or 350° would give a square line while 345° would be five degrees of port bias and 358° would be eight degrees of starboard bias. In practice, all you need to calculate is the bearing of wind for a square line, anything to the left will always make the port end favoured and vice versa.

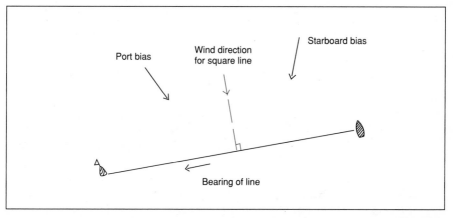

77 Numeric check for bias

If you are sailing on a yacht with reasonably sophisticated instruments, then you may have a display giving you the actual magnetic bearing of the wind while you are sailing along, but most of us are not so lucky and at best have instruments giving us the angle of the wind from the bow. In this case, the easiest way to find the wind direction in your pre-start manoeuvring is to slow each tack down as you go through head to wind and note the compass heading when the boom flaps amidships. Beware that you do not get confused as you approach the line for the final run in, as dirt from yachts to windward can temporarily shift the effective wind to give a misleading direction.

Tidal streams

When starting in an area with tidal streams or current there are several other considerations to make in deciding whereabouts on the line you want to start. However, if the stream is of even strength over the whole starting area then for most purposes it can be ignored by the competitor. The reasons behind this are explained further in the 'tidal wind' section in chapter 3, but in short, the wind you are sailing in will be modified by the tidal stream or current to give you a 'sailing wind'. Since this modification will be even over the starting area, you only need to look at the wind you are sailing in. It is the poor committee who are anchored and therefore do not experience the sailing wind who have to work it out.

The tidal stream will obviously affect the speed and ease with which you approach the line, but this is more of a tactical problem than a strategic one and so it is dealt with under starting tactics.

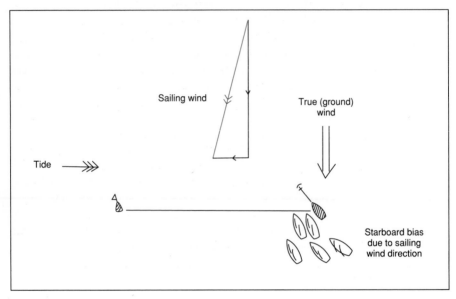

78 Use sailing wind to ascertain bias - not ground wind

There are lots of other situations when the tide does have to be taken into account at the start. Any time there is a difference in stream from one part of the line to another you have to consider the effect. Maybe there is more foul tide on one side of the course than the other, or possibly a counter current has started on one side while there is still foul tide elsewhere. These problems tend to be encountered more often when dealing with a fixed starting line rather than a committee-boat start since in the latter case the sensible committee will have chosen a place with weak or at least even streams for the line (see diagrams 79 – 80).

The Royal Yacht Squadron line at Cowes is a classic case where there is often a tidal difference from one end to the other. The normal line is a mile long and it stretches from close to the Isle of Wight all the way across the Solent to the edge of the Southampton Water shipping channel. For offshore races, the normal situation is to start the race as the tide is on the turn. This means that invariably there is a strong counter current close inshore on both shores with a foul stream in the middle of the line. Inevitably this causes bunching, especially at the port (Island) end of the line.

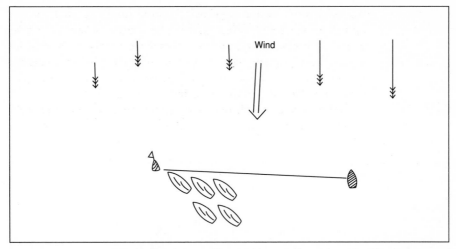

79 Less tide favours port end

The situation here is further complicated in that having started on starboard tack at the port end of the line, you then have to be able to tack onto port in order to avoid the rocks after only a very short distance. This can end with the leading boats being blocked by the majority of the fleet who are still coming in on starboard. Meantime, at the other end of the line yachts which started there have crossed the small area of foul tide and are now in counter current, probably with far fewer yachts to contend with. Moreover, you hit this shore on port tack and can always tack away since you are coming out on starboard.

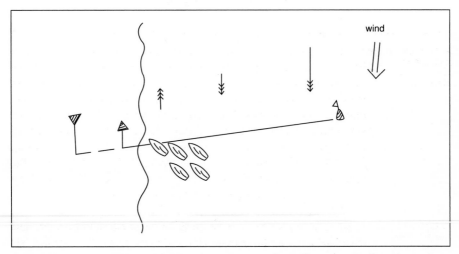

80 Inshore counter current favours port end

This type of line can get very complicated and often the options are not conclusive and so you see two separate fleets starting, one at either end. From a competitor's point of view this is not very satisfactory since either end has an element of gamble in its choice (see diagram 81).

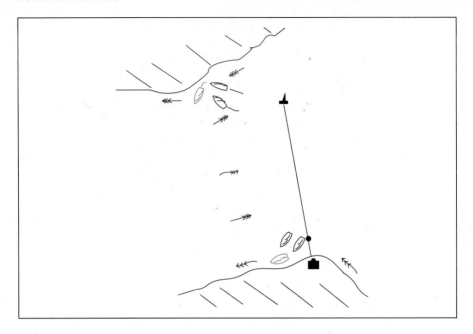

81 Starboard
shore is easier
for short tacking

Downwind starts

If the start is really downwind, with at least one gybe needed
before the first mark, then the strategy is very similar to that used
for upwind starts. Once again it is the bias of the line which is
critical, not the position of the first mark, although here you
obviously need to start at the downwind end of the line.

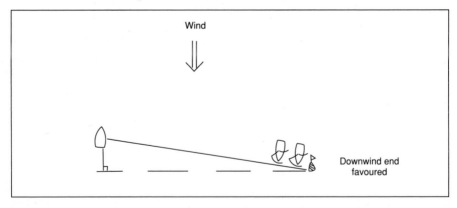

Wind

Downwind end
favoured

82 Downwind
start line - bias
is mirror image
of upwind

Boat-to-boat tactics can be quite different for running starts and
these are covered in chapter 10.

Reaching starts

Reaching starts give a totally different set of questions which need
addressing before the best position on the line can be determined.

The tidal considerations are more or less the same as for any other type of start. That is, find the area with the best current if there is any difference over the line, look for counter currents near the edges if you are close to shore, etc. Once again, the sailing wind will be affected by the current but as you are sailing in this modified wind it is not a subject for concern.

The chief difference between upwind/downwind starts and a reaching start is that in the latter case the actual distance to the first mark from different points on the line is important.

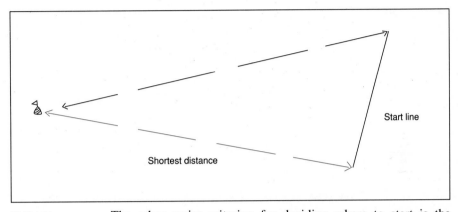

Start line

Shortest distance

83 Reaching
start - distance
to first mark is
important

The other major criterion for deciding where to start is the apparent wind angle on the reach. In some cases, for example if it is just about a spinnaker leg in gusty conditions, the windward end of the line will give you a faster point of sailing down the reach. In other conditions, it may be faster to start at the leeward end, particularly if the reach is quite broad. In either case you must also consider your size and speed of boat in relation to the rest of the fleet because there is no point in being in the 'right' place if you immediately get sailed over by other, bigger boats. This will be dealt with more fully under tactics.

84 Close reach
start - windward
end often best

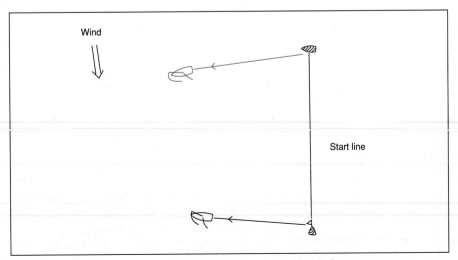

Wind

Start line

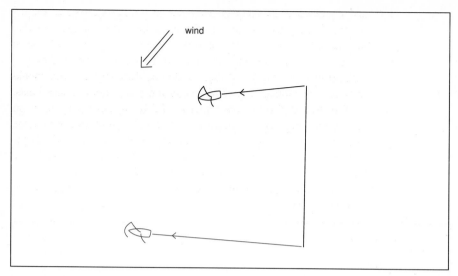

85 Broad reach
start - leeward
end usually best

So much for theory, but in practice the first mark may be a very long distance away indeed, maybe tens of miles away, in which case you may feel that the extra distance sailed from one end compared to the other is so small as to be immaterial. In fact, though, even if it is only one or two boat lengths' difference, this could be just enough to put you ahead and in clear air for the whole leg.

It is quite simple to plot the position of the line on a chart (or on a plotting sheet): put in the direction of the first leg and then simply measure the bias as in diagram 86.

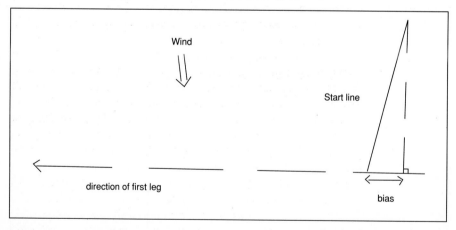

86 Bias on a
reaching start

Distance marks

Committees will often use inner and outer distance marks to limit where you are allowed to start and sometimes to protect the committee boat. There are two things which you need to realize about these distance marks.

One point is that distance marks normally count as starting marks and therefore you cannot claim water in the normal way at them - as long as they are 'on or near the line'. In practice this means that they need to be within about two boat lengths of the line to count in this way. If they are behind the line then they may be ignored totally, while if they are the course side of the line then normally you should treat them as ordinary rounding marks and give water to inside boats.

The second point is that under the IYRR, a yacht is racing from her preparatory (five-minute) signal and the limit marks become relevant from this time. This means that if one of the marks is far enough on the pre-course side to allow you to sail between it and the line, you are allowed to do this after the five-minute gun has gone and then sail further along the extension of the line as in the diagram below.

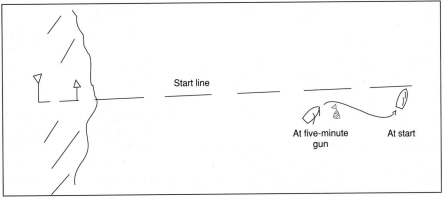

Start line

At five-minute gun

At start

87 Limit mark is relevant from the five-minute signal

It is not often that this ploy becomes useful, but I shall recount two occasions when I have used it to advantage in order to explain the situation fully.

During the 1989 Fastnet start, the line was, as usual, the Royal Yacht Squadron's western line with a channel buoy (West Bramble) as the outer distance. On this occasion the tide was still setting to the east when we started and this meant that the buoy was indeed on the pre-course side of the line - by about 20m. At the start time, there was going to be a foul tide everywhere on the line except at the extreme port end, but there would also be a counter current about 100m outside the line at the starboard end. The wind was light to non-existent but there was the beginnings of a sea breeze on the shore near the starboard end of the line.

On the Swan 53 I was on we decided to make use of the position of the starboard limit mark and were doing maximum speed under power with five minutes, one second to go. On a Swan 53 this means about nine knots! The engine was cut just before the five-minute signal and we coasted towards the new wind being careful to stay the pre-course side of the line at all times. By the start we had fair tide and some wind and went on to take a lead of several miles over the next boat in our class before they got into decent breeze.

Having got clear at the start we continued in the lead throughout the race until our mainsail split on the way back from the rock and we were forced to use the trysail for 120 miles - even then our lead was so great that we were only just pushed into second place!

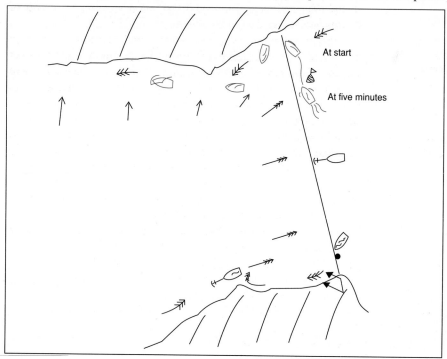

At start

At five minutes

88 Chacaboo's 1989 Fastnet start

Another example where it was possible and an advantage to go beyond the limit mark was at the start of the Solent race during the 1991 Admiral's Cup. Here it was the inner distance mark which had drifted to the pre-course side of the line and with starboard bias on the line we (*Wings of Oracle*), together with a handful of other yachts, manoeuvred between the five-minute gun and the start so that we eventually started right by the committee boat, 50m inside the limit mark.

89 1991 CMAC Solent race start

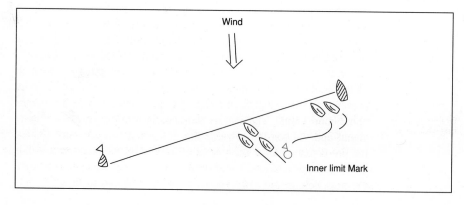

Wind

Inner limit Mark

You do have to be careful though, especially with the inner distance mark. Read the sailing instructions very carefully to see if the limit marks are described in detail. In some cases the committee forbids sailing between the distance mark and the committee boat *at any time* and this would obviously stop you using the sort of starting technique described above.

9.4
UPWIND

If you had a crystal ball which showed a picture of the beat over the time that it will take you to sail it and could identify where and when each wind shift was and where the best pressure was at any given moment, then in theory it should be possible to pick the best possible route up the beat. In practice we do not often sail with crystal balls (although maybe the French Admiral's Cup team had one in 1991). This means that we have to substitute good weather forecasting and a knowledge of the basic principles involved in lieu of this hypothetical aid.

Wind shifts upwind - general principles

The most important single factor to take into account when beating to windward is the shifting direction of the wind. Being on the right side of a shift can gain you vast amounts of distance, while being on the wrong side of the same shift can be very depressing. Diagram 90 shows why this is the case.

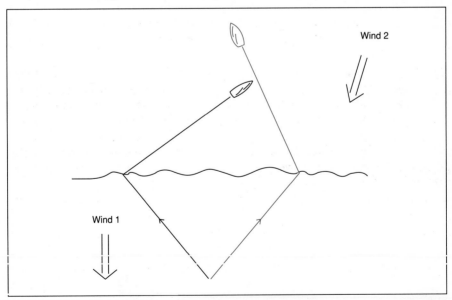

90 Effect of a single wind shift

I like to think of going upwind as if climbing a ladder. The purpose of the exercise is to get to the top (the windward mark) and the rungs of the ladder are perpendicular to the present wind direction. Thus, in order to decide how far up the beat we have got and whether another yacht is ahead or behind our own, we merely need to look at which 'rung of the ladder' the yachts are on and the one which is highest up the ladder is in front - at that time and assuming that the wind stays in the same direction.

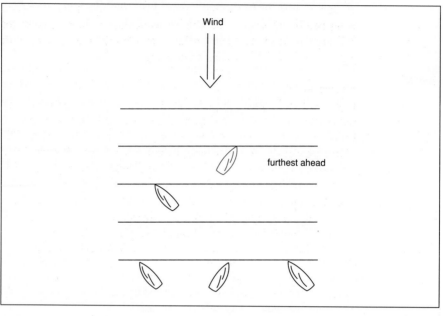

Whenever the wind changes direction, so the rungs of the ladder also move. This means that a wind shift effectively moves all the yachts either up or down the ladder depending on their positions, rather like a complicated game of snakes and ladders.

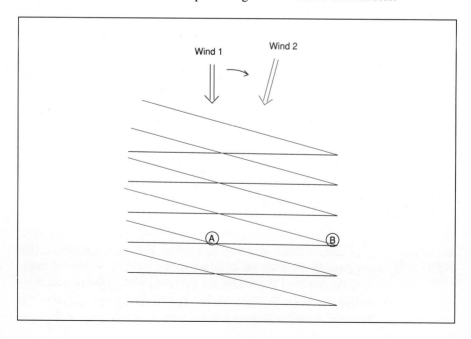

Sometimes the wind will shift quickly and then stay in the new direction, other times it may continually shift backwards and forwards (oscillating shift), while on yet another occasion it may gradually shift over a longer period of time (persistent shift or wind bend). In order to be able to work out the best strategy for a beat it is vital that you are able to identify the type of shift pattern with which you are contending.

Simple shifts

If you anticipate one simple shift at some stage up the beat, then the strategy is simple. Sail towards the expected shift, wait until it happens and then tack onto the newly lifted tack. This means that if you anticipate a shift which will veer the wind (move its direction clockwise) then you should sail on port tack, towards the right-hand side of the course until the shift occurs. Obviously you have to be careful not to go too far towards the layline in case you either overstand the windward mark after the shift or in case the shift never happens, but in essence this is a simple situation.

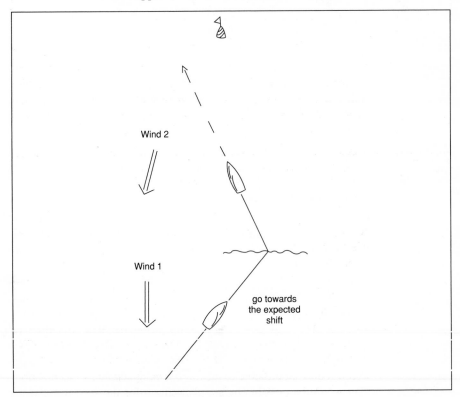

Wind 2

Wind 1

go towards
the expected
shift

93 Sail towards
a shift

Persistent shift or wind bend

If you think that the wind is going to shift gradually further and further in one direction during the beat (eg. the normal veer experienced in a sea breeze), then the situation is somewhat different.

In this case you must try to look ahead and anticipate the average wind direction up the whole beat and only tack when the wind has shifted beyond that point. For example, if the wind starts at 230° and is forecast to veer steadily to 260° by the end of the beat, this would put the mean wind at (260+230)/2 = 245°. You should not normally tack onto starboard until the wind has reached about this direction. Even if you got some tempting early shifts to, say, 240° you should refrain from tacking on them since you would eventually lose out as the wind goes further and further round.

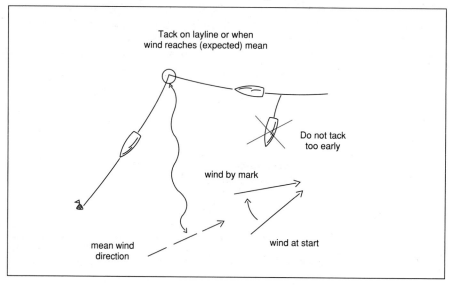

Tack on layline or when
wind reaches (expected) mean

Do not tack
too early

wind by mark

mean wind
direction

wind at start

94 Persistent
shift or wind
bend

The difficulty here is in trying to gauge the mean or average wind direction without the help of a crystal ball!

Oscillating wind shifts

It is most common for the wind to shift in an oscillating type of pattern, moving backwards and forwards around an average. In this case you want to be on whichever is the lifted tack at any given time - relative to the mean direction.

In the case of an oscillating wind, there is often a pattern to the oscillations. You may find for example that the oscillations happen over a regular time scale, with maybe a shift every five or 10 minutes. If you can identify a pattern like this then it obviously helps considerably in deciding on your short-term strategy. If it is known or anticipated that the wind is about to shift back again, it may be possible to tack into a more advantageous position than would be possible by simply waiting for the shift to happen.

As can be seen from the study of polar curves in diagram 95, when the wind is oscillating and we are able to sail on the lifted tack then our boat should be set up for slightly more speed and less pointing than would be normal in a steady wind. This is to enable the yacht to be always moving as fast as possible towards the next shift and such that she is performing to give the best velocity towards the mark (VMC) at all times.

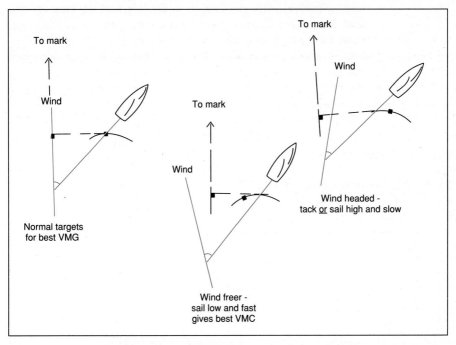

To mark

Wind

Normal targets for best VMG

To mark

Wind

Wind freer - sail low and fast gives best VMC

To mark

Wind

Wind headed - tack or sail high and slow

95 Maximise VMC in a oscillating wind

Complicated shift patterns

In many race situations there is not a simple either persistent shift or oscillating shift pattern but a combination of both types of shift. Going back to the sea breeze example, although the sea breeze will normally veer as the day goes on, there will be considerable oscillations within this overall persistent shift, especially early on in the day. The principle is still the same, however, it is the average wind direction for the remainder of the beat which is crucial - if on a lift compared to the average then stay on that tack, if on a header compared to this average then tack.

Leebowing the tide

In chapter 3 we looked at tidal wind and it became apparent that one of the chief effects of the tide changing direction was a corresponding change in the sailing wind. If beating in a cross-tide situation this fact can often be used to good advantage.

While the tide stays constant there is no particular advantage in being on one tack or the other (from a tidal point of view) because it is only as the tide changes that it causes a wind shift. It is worth looking at the real effect that a tide change has on the wind in order to be able to decide how best to deal with it. This is shown in diagram 96 where it can be seen that as the tide starts to change, there will be a gradual shift which will continue until the tide has built up to its maximum rate in the new direction. The sailing wind will then stay constant until the next turn of the tide when the reverse gradual shift will happen as the tide first slackens off and then turns. This diagram assumes for simplicity's sake that there is no other reason for the wind to shift. In this slightly simplified case, it would be true to say that you should *leebow* the tide since this would make maximum use of the wind shifts.

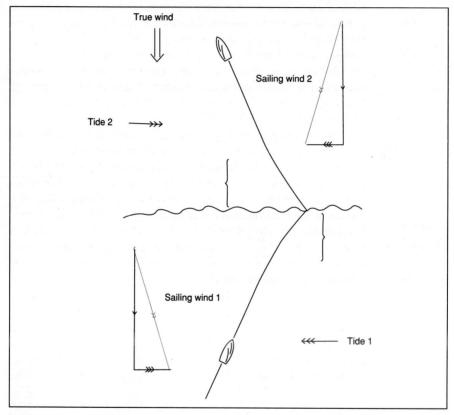

96 Leebowing the tide

Thus, it can be seen that if we consider a beat with one or more full tides followed by only part of a tide as the windward mark is reached, any full period of tide can be considered as an oscillation whereas the last period of tide may need to be considered as a persistent shift. As normal, it is the *average* wind direction over the whole beat (or the remainder of the beat once you have started it) which is important.

If there are other reasons for the wind to shift apart from the changes in the tide then these need to be superimposed on the changes caused by the tide to get an overall pattern. Sometimes this will enhance the leebow effect, while at other times it may nullify it. The navigator has to make the best forecast of the overall changes to the sailing wind in order to offer the most accurate advice on strategy.

Limiting your exposure

Most of the above comments have been written as if you were on your own during the beat, merely trying to reach the windward mark as fast as possible. In reality, you will normally be sailing against other yachts and, especially in one-design racing, your real goal is to reach the windward mark faster than anyone else rather than as fast as possible. This subject is covered in detail in chapter 10 on tactics, but it is worth saying here that you must be aware of your competitors and at least take note of their strategy because if they all disagree with you then it is at least possible that your forecasting or interpretation is wrong.

Even without the pressure of direct competitors to limit how far you are prepared to go in extreme directions, it is normally worth trying to sail reasonably conservatively and avoid getting to laylines too early or putting your position at risk if your forecast does prove to be wrong.

I used to advocate sailing in 'cones' up the beat to limit how far off the rhumb line you went but gradually came to realize that this put artificial limits on your strategy. I still believe that in the absence of a good forecast, it is worth staying within say a 30° cone down wind from the mark but must emphasize very strongly that this should only be taken as an approximate guide and if you have a valid reason for going further than this away from the rhumb line then do not feel inhibited simply because of the existence of a 'cone'.

97 Use of limiting sectors to reduce exposure

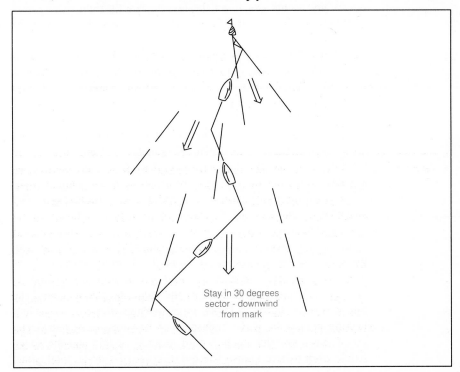

Stay in 30 degrees sector - downwind from mark

Your strategy as you approach the windward mark is often affected by the actions and positions of other yachts, and the tactical side is covered in the next chapter. However, it is worth looking at the overall strategy assuming that you are approaching the mark alone, because this does sometimes happen, especially in longer offshore races.

Approach in an oscillating wind

If the wind is oscillating then it is important not to get onto the layline too early or it will not be possible to utilize any later shifts and you may find yourself being forced to approach the mark on a header. However, from the crew's point of view it is much easier if there is enough approach time to allow the spinnaker pole to be got ready. In most situations the spinnaker itself will have been prepared on the previous tack while the gear was on the 'high' side.

Approach along the shore, against the tide

One of the classic difficulties for the navigator arises when the beat is against the tide and it has been possible to tack along the shore in relatively weak current. The dilemma is in deciding when to leave the shore: too early and it will be necessary to put in a tack out in the strong current which is always disastrous, too late and you will end up reaching in to the mark and will have lost out to any yachts which get the layline exactly right.

When coaching I often hear: 'whenever we tack out from the shore the wind always seems to head us'. If you consider the point, the wind will normally decrease and maybe will also be headed as you sail from the shore out into the stronger current. This is because the sailing wind will be changed as shown in chapter 3. If you know the relative strengths of the current both where you are presently sailing and what it will be further offshore, then it should be possible to calculate (approximately) how much the wind will be changed by the increased stream. This means that not only do you need to allow an offset for the actual drift of the tide but also an angular offset to compensate for the shift in the sailing wind. Failing to take both factors into account is the prime reason why so many people find this situation difficult. It is worth looking at one hypothetical example to illustrate the necessary workings.

Consider beating along a shore against 0.5 knots of tide with the sailing wind blowing at 30° to the tidal stream inshore and is registering as 240° and eight knots. The windward mark is out in the main channel and as soon as the shoreline is left behind the tide will increase to 2.5 knots. In eight knots of wind the yacht's tacking angle is 85° with a boat speed of 5.5 knots, while at anything below 6.5 knots this angle would increase to 95° and the speed would drop to five knots. The question is what is the total offset to allow for the tide in order to judge the layline correctly?

a) As can be seen from diagram 98, the 1-in-60 rule would indicate that the offset from true wind to sailing wind must be about two degrees (60 / 8 x 0.5 x 0.5).

b) Out in the main stream the same rules would show that the sailing wind will be offset by 10° (60 / 8 x 2.5 x 0.5), thus the wind will be backed a further eight degrees as the yacht sails out into the tide.

c) This means that the new sailing wind direction will be (240 - 8)= 232°.

d) The sailing wind will also reduce in strength to only just over six knots, so the speed will be five knots and the tacking angle will increase to 90°.

e) With a sailing wind of 232° the heading of the yacht on starboard tack will be (232-45)= 187°.

f) The course to steer in order to allow for the tidal stream will need to be approximately (60 / 5 x 2.5)= 30° offset into the tidal stream, so the layline will need to be 30° further along the coast than normal.

g) The layline will therefore be reached when the buoy is bearing (187-30)= 157°.

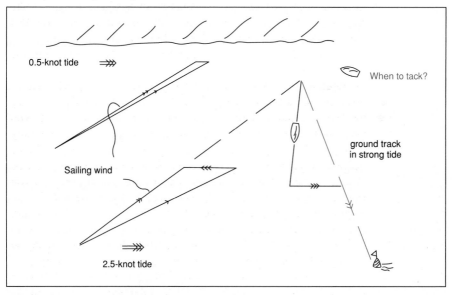

0.5-knot tide ⇒⟫

When to tack?

Sailing wind

ground track
in strong tide

2.5-knot tide

98 Complicated layline calculation

This sort of calculation looks very complex but if done in a real situation and taken one step at a time it becomes relatively straightforward and should not put a reasonably numerate navigator off. It should also be realized that it is not necessary to work the whole thing out to any great degree of accuracy, it is the principle and an approximation of the right answer which is important.

Rhumb-line sailing

In the absence of any information to make you suppose that conditions might change, it is usually best to stick to the rhumb line since this gives the shortest course to sail. If in a cross-tidal situation, the rhumb line must obviously be modified to take the tide into account and should be the overall course to steer allowing for all predicted tide.

If it is expected that the next mark will be reached with a strong cross tide, then it may well be worth aiming to arrive a little up-tide of the mark just in case the wind falls light or a mistake was made in the navigation. This used to be very important for offshore races in the days before accurate fixing equipment but is less so nowadays.

Out of the current

If the reaching leg is against the current or tidal stream and if it is possible to get out of the worst of the foul current then this will obviously pay. This is the situation experienced when sailing along a coastline, normally there will be less current near the shore and most in the deep water (except around headlands and localized shallow patches).

It is essential to consider the gain to be made by sailing out of the current against any potential losses associated with this. Maybe there will be less wind along the shore, or maybe it will add a considerable distance to the course to be sailed. It is nearly always going to be possible to quantify both the gains and losses and compare them to ascertain the net effect and this is the right approach to take.

Lyme Bay, on England's south coast, for example, stretches for 50 miles from Portland Bill in the east to Start Point in the west. There is less and less tide as you progress deeper into the bay, but in all but the lightest conditions it is not worth going more than two-three miles north of the direct route from headland to headland. This is because, after an initial significant drop in the rate of the tidal stream as soon as you are inside the line between headlands, the tidal gradient further in to the bay is very slight until you are right up the beach.

99 Against the current - tidal gains must outweigh extra distance sailed

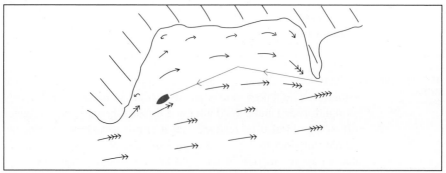

When it is best to sail high first

There are going to be lots of times when your forecast of the wind indicates that it will change during a reaching leg. This not only applies offshore but also inshore, especially if there is a particular cloud formation visible or it is known that there is a geographical reason to produce a wind change. On these occasions it is obviously important to be able to consider the implications of the impending wind change and modify your strategy accordingly.

Because most yachts will be fastest at closer reaching angles in lighter winds and wider angles as the wind increases, it is best to sail high for the first part of a reach if the forecast indicates that either:
a) the wind is going to increase at some time further down the leg, or
b) the wind is going to head later.

100 When to sail high initially

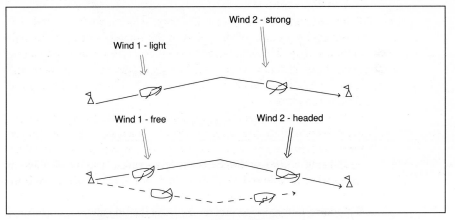

When it is best to sail low first

The converse to the above is obviously also true. If the wind is forecast to decrease or to free later on then it will often pay to sail low at the start of the reach, so that when the wind has changed it is then possible to maintain good speeds by sailing higher angles.

101 When to sail low initially

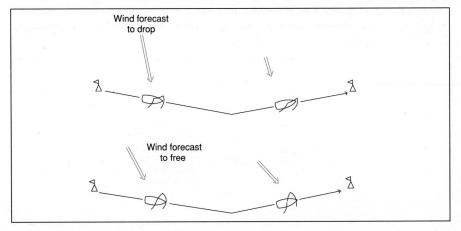

Use of best VMC when reaching

The best VMC is literally 'the optimum velocity made good along the course' in a given set of conditions. This gives the theoretically best course to sail at any given moment as shown in diagram 102. This optimum VMC can be found either from an accurate set of performance data for a yacht or by trial and error, or more realistically from a combination of the two methods, using the speed polar curves as a starter and then experimenting a little either side of the theoretical angle.

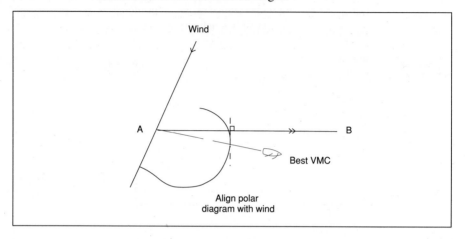

102 Best VMC
when reaching

If using a GPS or Decca set to give you a readout of VMC it must be remembered that this does not take future tides into account and will therefore not give the optimum even if you adjust the course to maximize this readout. As the tide altered, you would have to keep changing the course steered to keep the present reading of VMC at its best and as we saw in chapter 2 this is not a fast way to sail. VMC needs to be taken along the tidally corrected 'course to steer line', so if you want to use a fixing device to give you a real answer you need to put an imaginary waypoint into the machine along this line.

103 VMC in a
cross tide

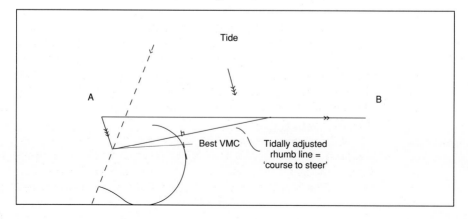

Weather routeing

Weather routeing as used by most of the Whitbread and BOC round-the-world racers in one form or another is the logical extension of the above idea. In principle it uses the idea of optimum VMC in the present conditions and then puts in the likely weather changes and gradually builds up a picture to give the optimum course(s) all the way to the next mark. Even by today's standards this takes a lot of computing power to achieve and, while it is possible to solve with on-board computers, the biggest problems ultimately tend to be errors in forecasting. This subject is covered in a little more detail in chapter 7 but is really outside the scope of this book.

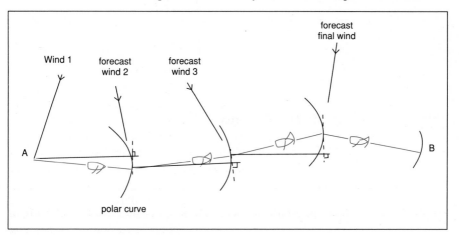

104 VMC for routeing - simplified diagram

Reach turning to a beat

We have considered what to do if the wind is going to head a little and as previously stated it is often best to sail a bit high in these circumstances. However, if the wind is forecast to head so much that what starts out as a reach will eventually turn into a beat, then the situation is somewhatdifferent. Incidentally, it is worth pointing out that by 'changing into a beat' I mean changing such that it will be necessary to tack in order to lay the mark regardless of whether you sailed high or low to start with.

In this case the leg should be considered in two more or less separate parts, the initial reaching bit and the latter beat. In general terms, the reach should be sailed as normal, optimizing VMC to get as far as possible along the reach and towards the next mark as possible at any time. Then, once it is no longer possible to lay the next mark, treat the remainder of the leg just like any other beat (see diagram 105).

The temptation for most people is to sail high 'so that it is not so much of a beat later' - well, a beat is a beat wherever you start from. The thinking of some others is to treat the reach in the same way as you would treat a beat and to sail towards the expected shift, that is sail low to start with. This can have some advantages, especially towards the end of the reaching section with a steady shift of the wind. Sailing somewhat low when you can still just fetch the mark will probably optimize VMC at that time.

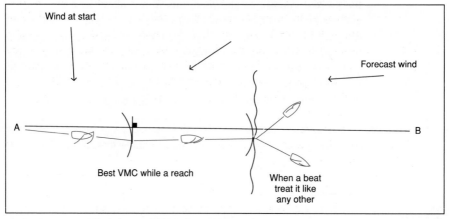

105 Reach becoming a beat

Reach turning into a run

The same definition applies here as in the last section. A reach only turns into a run if all yachts will end up having to gybe in order to get to the next mark even if they tried to take action to avoid this earlier.

Once again the leg should be considered in two separate sections, the reach and then the run. As soon as the wind has shifted enough so that you are sailing within your normal downwind angles, the remainder of the leg should be treated in exactly the same way as any other run, but until then simply sail to get as near to the mark as possible.

106 Reach becoming a run

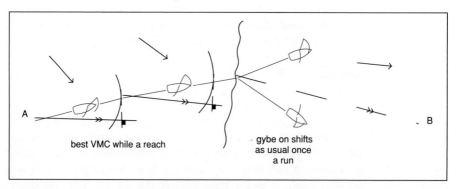

**9.7
THE GYBE
MARK**

In the absence of other yachts, rounding the gybe mark should be a fairly straightforward affair. Ideally the approach would be made slightly wide to allow the gybe itself to have been completed as the boat reaches the mark, allowing the new course to be set immediately.

If going from a close reach to a broad reach or run it may be necessary to peel spinnakers, in this case after the gybe. If the converse is true and the course changes from a broad reach to a close reach, then any peel should be done before the mark is reached.

If the wind is changeable or there is a possibility of the tidal stream altering as the mark is approached, beware of ending up too low for the buoy. It is very slow to have to drop the spinnaker and set a genoa for the final few boat lengths, especially as the spinnaker will probably need to be repacked and hoisted again on the new gybe as soon as the mark has been rounded. It is much safer if your final approach to the buoy is a very close reach to leave just a touch in hand.

The difficulties at the gybe mark stem chiefly from the presence of other yachts and various tactical situations which are likely to arise are dealt with in chapter 10.

Laylines

**9.8
THE LEEWARD
MARK**

As at the gybe mark, the leeward mark is relatively simple until there are other yachts to contend with. The chief aim will be to get the layline coming into the mark correct so that you neither need to put in a final panic gybe nor reach hard into the buoy.

If the gybing angles have been observed as you progress down the run, this should not present too many problems, unless the wind has changed dramatically since the last gybe. As a very approximate guide, the yacht will actually head straight down the windex arrow when on the other gybe (as long as the apparent wind speed and boat speed are more or less the same). The tidal stream needs to be taken into account with a reverse of the normal course shaping triangle in the same way as deciding on the layline while beating.

107 Gybing
angles downwind

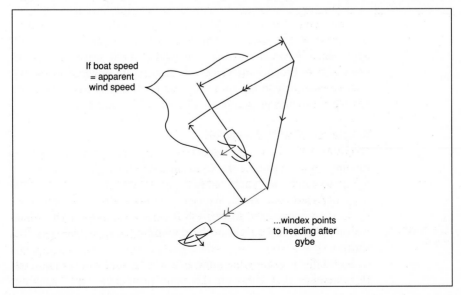

If boat speed = apparent wind speed

...windex points to heading after gybe

As a general principle, go for a slightly early layline call if the current is taking you towards the mark because you will not lose much by running a bit square in this situation, while if the opposite is true and the tide is setting you onto the mark it is safer to gybe somewhat late and risk over-standing slightly since to be running square against the tide will be very slow.

Which layline

In most cases it will be tactics that decide which is the best layline for your final approach to the mark. If getting an inside overlap is going to be important then this is likely to override most strategic considerations. There will be times, however, when it is possible to pick and choose and in this case it is usually better to pick the layline which allows a simple rounding rather than necessitating a float drop.

If the wind has shifted very far then it may mean that the favoured layline gives the more difficult rounding. In this case the crew need to be well prepared either to do an early drop and clear up before the mark or a float drop depending on the wind strength and on whether the tide is with or against you.

The same as upwind

**9.9
RUNNING
DOWNWIND**

As has been seen vividly in chapter 6, all yachts have optimum gybing angles downwind in the same way as they have optimum tacking angles upwind. Although it is physically possible to sail dead downwind, it rarely pays to do so. In wind strengths where the speed polar curves would indicate that this will not lose any speed, control problems normally prevent the yacht being sailed too square anyway.

Assuming that we are talking about real running, to a buoy so far downwind that it is necessary to gybe in order to lay the mark, then most of the strategy which applies to beating upwind will apply equally when running downwind. Wind shifts should be dealt with in broadly the same way as they are upwind, as should tidal streams and so on. In a way that is all that needs to be said, but the following paragraphs will look at this in more detail.

Simple wind shift downwind

Diagram 108 shows the effect of a simple wind shift while running. In this example the wind shifted to the right and, as when going upwind, the yacht which was to the right as the shift happened came out ahead. We can therefore deduce from this that if the wind is expected to veer (shift clockwise, to the right), then we should sail to the right of the rhumb line in anticipation of the shift.

So far this is exactly the same as it was upwind, but is important to remember that although the same principles apply running downwind actually gives a mirror image of the situation when beating. This means that while it is true to say that whether going upwind or downwind one should sail to the right if expecting a shift to the right (and vice versa), this will mean sailing towards the expected shift when going upwind and *away* from the shift when running downwind.

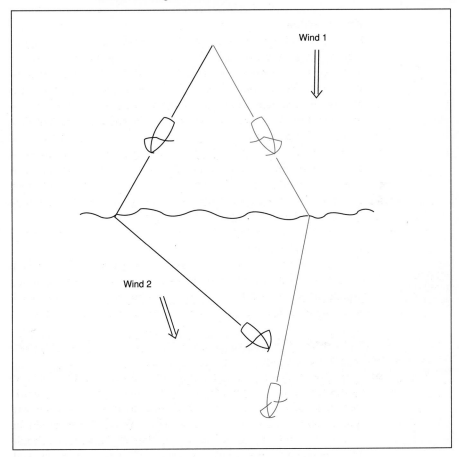

Wind 1

Wind 2

108 Effect of wind shift downwind

Oscillating shifts downwind

The principle of utilizing shifts downwind is to attempt to use each shift to stay pointing towards the leeward mark as much as possible. This means that if the wind is oscillating around a mean direction, each time it is to the right of the mean you should be on port gybe and vice versa when the wind is to the left of the mean direction (see diagram 109).

As with upwind sailing, a study of polar curves indicates that it is better to sail slightly high and fast while going towards a shift in a header, partly in order to get to the new wind faster and partly in order to maximize the VMC; while it is better to sail a little squarer than usual if forced to stay in a freer (see diagram 110).

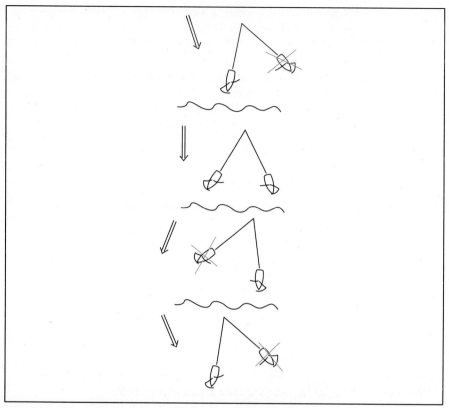

109 Use of shifts downwind

Wind bend or persistent shift downwind

110 Sail low in a freer; high and fast in a header

Once again the principle is the same as it is for upwind sailing. If going into a wind bend or if there is a persistent shift gradually going further and further in the same direction, it is vital to sail into the shift until the 'mean' wind is experienced. Judging where

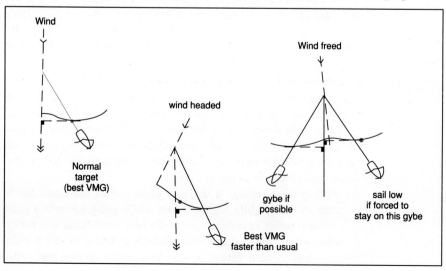

the mean is, is as always the hard thing to do and a crystal ball would come in very handy.

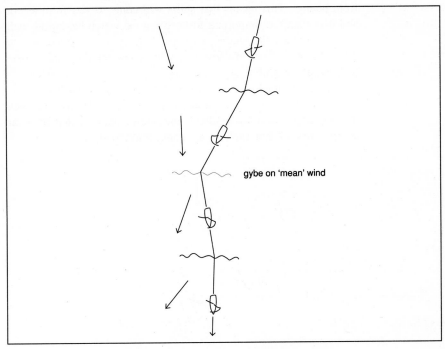

111 Persistent shift or wind bend - downwind

Oscillating shifts with an underlying trend

Very often even if the wind appears to be oscillating, a slightly deeper or longer-term investigation will show a persistent trend one way or the other. This is exemplified by a typical sea-breeze day when the wind will tend to veer during the day but, especially early on, there will be some major oscillations.

In this situation it is once again the mean wind for the leg that is important. If it is possible to establish what the mean is going to be, any shift to the right of this forecast average should see you on port gybe and any shifts which put the wind to the left of the mean should see you gybing onto starboard.

112 Oscillating shift with an underlying trend

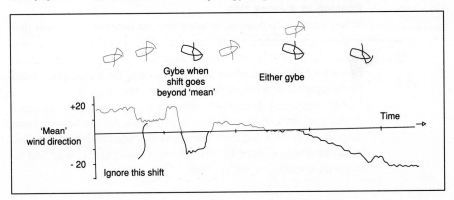

Looking for shifts when running

One difficulty when running is that the wind is, by definition, coming from behind. This means that shifts will come to you from astern and it is therefore important to keep a good watch behind as well as ahead. Since the tendency of most crews is to concentrate on the situation in front of them it may be worth detailing one person to look aft for shifts.

Another problem when compared to beating is that since it is physically possible to sail at any angle you like downwind (even if some are slower than others) the angles being sailed by your competitors are not such an accurate guide to shifts.

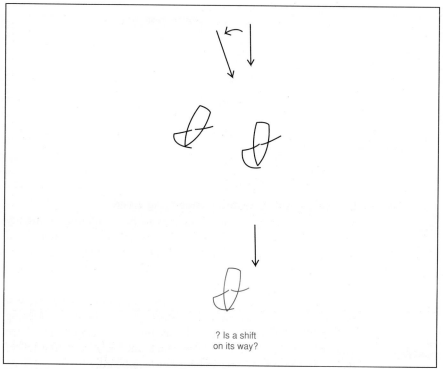

? Is a shift
on its way?

113 Judging
shift is hard
when running

Running in a cross tide

When we were looking at strategy upwind it became apparent that any advantage gained by the 'leebow' effect of the tide was caused by the wind shift in the sailing wind every time the tide turned. Downwind the same effect will be true and tidal changes should be thought of as wind shifts in just the same way.

Although most downwind sailing is a mirror image of upwind, in this case the leebow principle is still valid. As can be seen from diagram 113, the wind shift caused by the tide turning means that in the absence of other factors affecting the strategy, it is best to run with the tide on the lee side.

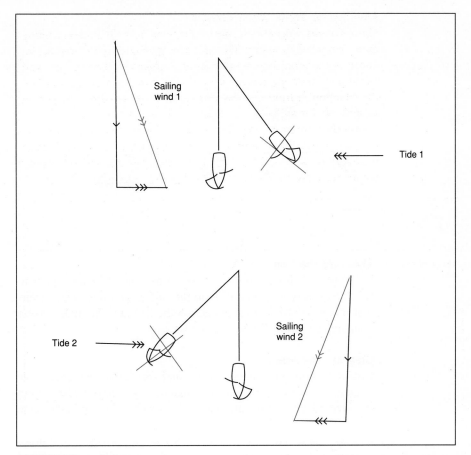

114 Leebowing
the tide
downwind

Identify the line

**9.10
THE FINISH**

The finish line is not always easy to see from a long distance and it is really important to identify it as early as possible. In important races there are often spectator boats clustered around the line which might make it difficult to see, or the committee boat in use may well be much smaller than that used for starting.

Favoured end of the line

From a strategic point of view, the most important thing to consider about the finish is what part of the line is favoured.

With an upwind start line we saw that as long as the tide was even over the whole line then the favoured end was the one which was furthest upwind. The finishing line is a mirror image of the starting line and if approaching it on a beat then, all other things being equal, it will be quickest to finish at the downwind end.

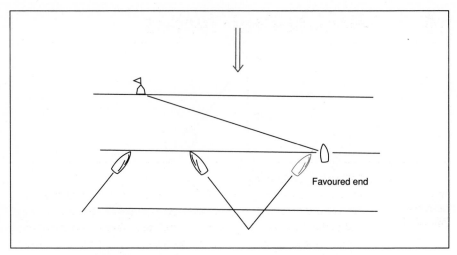

Favoured end

115 Finish-line
bias

Shooting the line

In the final approach to the finishing line it nearly always pays to
finish as nearly at right angles to the line as possible. This means
that it is usually best to shoot across the line at right angles, using
your momentum to drive you across.

Clearing the line

Unless the sailing instructions state otherwise, it is always acceptable
to clear the line in either direction and once you have finished (and
received a finishing signal) there is no need to carry on in the same
direction as that in which you approached the finish line. This can
be quite important if there is a strong foul tide which would make
carrying on to clear the line difficult or slow - it should be remembered
that you are still racing and therefore subject to the racing rules
until you have finished and cleared the line.

10   Boat-To-Boat Tactics

Definition of tactics

There are many ways of defining tactics. In this chapter I mean
the various ways of dealing with boat-to-boat situations so as to
make the best use of the rules and to enhance your strategic
decisions whenever possible. As well as the one-to-one situations,
we shall also consider the way that overall fleet tactics play an
important role, especially in one-design or level-rating types of
racing.

As with strategy in the previous chapter, it is simplest and most
convenient to look at each leg of the course in turn and consider
the appropriate tactics, so that is how the chapter will be
organized.

Tactics or strategy?

In a lot of cases the tactics of a situation will conflict with the
planned strategy. In these cases it is important to be able to recognize
the differences between the two and to be able to put priorities
on each.

In quite a number of cases it will be possible to use tactical
situations to 'persuade' the opposition to follow your own strategy,
if you want to keep tabs on them. At other times you will be able
to force the opposition to go the opposite way to that which you
consider best if you either want to force them into a less
advantageous position or are just not concerned about them and
want room to make your own decisions.

Importance of the rules

In order to be able to make use of or even survive any boat-to-
boat situations it is vital that you have a thorough knowledge and
understanding of the racing rules. These are contained in a booklet
published by the International Yacht Racing Union. The National
Authority in each country (the RYA in Britain) publishes its own
versions of the rules and these will contain specific local
variations. As well as the official rule books, there are always a
handful of books which are designed to help the user with
understanding and interpreting the rules. As can be imagined,
some of these are excellent while others are less good.

Fleet sailing

Most racing and certainly all one-design or level-rating events are far more about sailing against the rest of the fleet than they are about trying to finish as fast as possible. This philosophy does not necessarily apply to handicap races where there may not be other yachts with similar ratings to your own.

Assuming, then, that we are looking at racing where the actual finishing time is of less relevance than the finishing order, there are some basic tactical considerations which will need to be borne in mind at all times.

In these circumstances it is best to sail conservatively and not to take excessive risks. For example, if your strategy is to go to the left up a beat in anticipation of an anti-clockwise wind shift, then only go as far to the left as is necessary to be on the favoured side of the majority of the fleet. If you are certain that the shift is going to be of benefit and think that your knowledge is not shared by the others then you may go *just* to the left of the whole fleet. If, on the other hand, you are fairly happy with the strategy but think that everyone else is following the same line, there is rarely any virtue in going further towards the shift than the middle of the fleet.

Try to think in terms of your position relative to the opposition rather than a position in isolation and you will often find that this modifies your strategy considerably.

Obviously, there will be times when you have either got split from the rest of the fleet or when you are convinced that they are all wrong and you have a chance to make real gains by going the other way. In the former case then, fine, make use of the situation as best you can. In the latter case just be aware of what you are doing and realize that taking a flier is normally a last-resort measure when you do not feel able to compete on even terms with the rest or for some reason are near the back of the fleet. Do not blame the flier for a later bad result - if the flier loses you places then it was your decision which was bad.

In my experience, the consistently well-placed yachts in any one-design fleet get their results by gently plugging away at the opposition and generally making less mistakes than their competitors, not by taking fliers.

**10.2
PRE-START**

This is a very short section but none the less important for that. Officially, racing rules come into play at the preparatory signal (five-minute gun) but in practice the serious racer will be thinking about his position long before that time.

Timed runs

By the time the five-minute gun has gone, decisions about where to start must have been made, at least in principle. Not only the strategy needs to be worked out by now, but also the timing of the actual start needs to have been thought about and probably practised so that the effects of tidal streams, etc., on the run in to the line can have been ascertained.

In a lot of cases it will be worth doing realistic practice starts, timing your approach from a repeatable position and improving the approach until you know just where you will want to be as the time to the real start comes up. In doing this try not to be too fixed in your approach, it is rare for a particular practice run to be exactly repeatable at the real start since there will inevitably be other yachts in the way during the latter. A feel for approximate positions and distances is what is required.

Think about the opposition

When making your strategic decisions on where to start you will need to think about the rest of the fleet. For example, there is little point starting at the port end on starboard if your yacht is the smallest in the fleet and will immediately get sailed over by the rest. Similarly, there is no gain to be had by starting next to a large masthead racing yacht which can point like a witch if you are sailing a small fractional cruiser/racer with somewhat less pointing capabilities. Think about how your yacht fits into the fleet structure during the pre-start and modify your strategy accordingly.

Spatial awareness

It is very noticeable on a start line that there are some yachts which seem to be able to get into the right place at the right time while others, although probably understanding where they would like to be, always end up in the second or third row.

One of the major reasons for this seeming disparity is that some people appear to have better spatial awareness than others. Those who either have this awareness naturally or who have developed it as a specific skill will be able to call for the helmsman to go up or down and for the trimmers to accelerate or slow down while taking into account the yachts all around them. The less skilled among us will not have this advantage and will struggle to get somewhere near the line without being premature.

For the latter sailors it is worthwhile practising manoeuvring in tight situations, ideally with other yachts playing the same game and one sure way to improve this skill is to take part in match racing. Here, an awareness of where your opponent and how long it will take to sail to the line is vital if pre-start control is going to be achieved.

The rules applicable to starting

10.3 AT THE START

a) Luffing rights: Once the preparatory signal has gone and the fleet is subject to the racing rules, yachts are allowed to luff others within certain limits.

Before starting and clearing the line, the chief limitation is that you must always luff slowly and in such a way as to give the other party room and opportunity to keep clear. There is no 'proper course' until the start gun has gone and so until this time you are allowed to luff as far as head to wind as long as you have 'luffing rights'.

When the windward yacht is forward of the mast abeam position then the leeward yacht is only allowed to luff as far as close hauled.These rules have important ramifications for how to

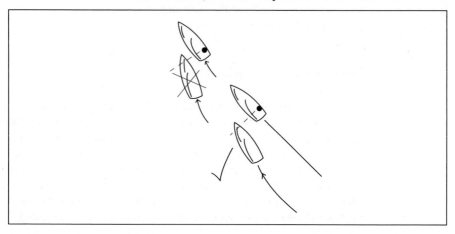

116 Luffing from behind mast abeam - before the start

make space (legally) at the start. For example, if a yacht reaches in from behind and to leeward of another, the windward yacht must respond to a luff up to a close-hauled course but the leeward yacht must give ample time for the windward yacht to respond.

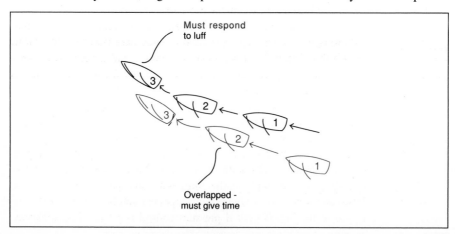

Must respond to luff

Overlapped - must give time

117 Luffing before the start

This means that it is possible to put your bow into a small gap, and as long as ample time is allowed, the gap should open up to allow you in - as long that is as the boat to leeward of the gap does not luff to keep you out!

b) Barging: Unlike the situation at other marks, the rules governing starting marks are covered totally separately by rule 42. In basic terms this says that if the starting mark is surrounded by clear water then outside yachts are not obliged to give room to those inside.

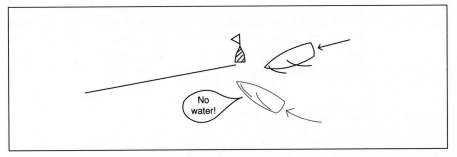

118 Barging

This means that if you have decided to start at the starboard end of the line and want to hover there head to wind blocking the passage of other yachts, this is fine. Also on your final approach to the line, there is no need to give any room to yachts who are trying to barge in to windward of you.

c) Water after the starting signal: There is an exception to the above rule, however, and it is one which causes a lot of grief at starboard-biased starts. Rule 42 goes on to say: 'after the starting signal the leeward yacht shall not deprive a windward yacht of room at such a mark by sailing either: (a) to windward of the compass bearing of the course to the next mark or (b) above close hauled.'

This little clause is often overlooked by less experienced racers who continue to luff almost head to wind to keep barging yachts out. As the rule so clearly states, once the starting signal has gone you must bear away to either a close-hauled course or to the bearing for the first mark if to do otherwise would shut a competitor out.

119 Assume proper course at the start

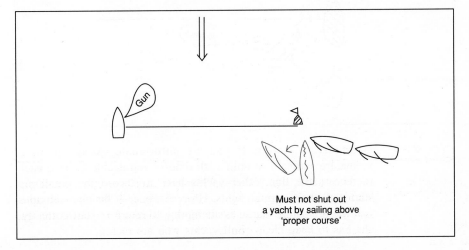

Must not shut out a yacht by sailing above 'proper course'

d) When the mark is not surrounded by navigable water: If the starting mark is not surrounded by navigable water, then normal rules for giving water at obstructions will apply and, in general terms, water must be given to inside yachts.

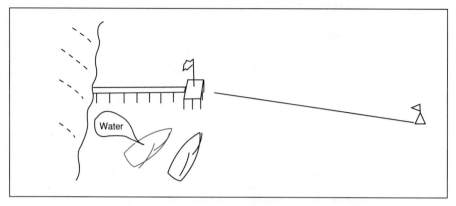

120 When starting mark is not surrounded by navigable water

e) Water to tack at starting marks: One other point to be aware of in your final approach to the line is that rule 43.3.a. specifically denies yachts the right to call for water to tack when approaching a starting mark (or its ground tackle). This means that, especially in a situation with a foul tide, you have to be very careful not to get boxed into a position where you need to tack in order to clear one end of the line.

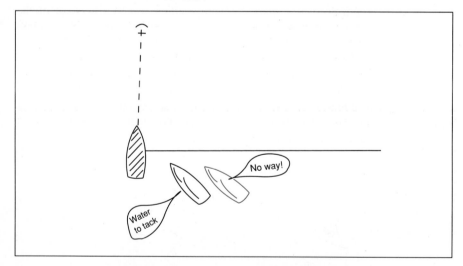

121 No rights to water to tack

f) Premature starter: If you are unfortunate enough to be a premature starter then until such time as you decide to head back to recross the line, other yachts have to accord the premature starter all their normal rights. However, once it becomes obvious that the premature starter is attempting to return to start correctly, she has to keep clear of all yachts who are racing.

As soon as the premature starter has returned fully to the pre-start side of the line, she suddenly reacquires all her normal rights - but if this gives her right of way over another yacht then, because it is a transitional rule, she must give the other yacht ample time and opportunity to keep clear.

Starboard-end starts

When strategy decides that the starboard end of the line is favoured, either because of bias or for any other reason, then the tactician must look in detail at what is required. There will normally be one (and only one) yacht which is able to get the perfect start, at the committee boat, going at full speed and on the line as the gun goes. Everyone else will have to compromise in one way or another. Some yachts will start further down the line but still in the front row while others may be later at the line but still right at the committee-boat end. The best compromise will depend on the strategy after the start itself.

a) Starboard end and starboard side of beat: In a situation where not only is the starboard end of the line favoured but also the starboard side of the first beat, it will be of paramount importance to be able to tack onto port as soon as possible after the start. In this case it will not matter too much if you are not in the front row as the gun goes but being right next to the committee boat will make a significant difference. Unless you are sure that you are able to get the 'best' start, it will therefore often pay to plan to arrive just a little late, maybe by one boat length or so. If all went really well, then you could still find yourself being in the pole position, but if your calculations are slightly wrong then at least you will be able to tack very soon after the gun, as soon as you have clear air from the 'best starter'.

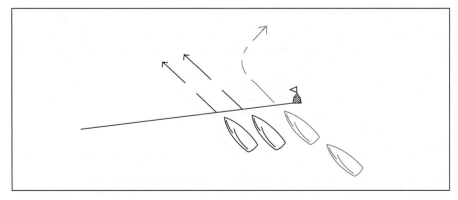

122 Starboard bias and starboard side of beat

b) Starboard end but port side of beat: The opposite situation to that described above is where the line is biased to favour the starboard end but the strategy for the first beat is to favour the left side of the course. In this case the most important consideration will be to come off the starting line in clear air and not to be forced to tack off to get out of dirt.

Thus, the best solution is to be prepared to start a little way down the line and not to worry too much about being right at the starboard end. In this situation, timing is much more critical than exact positioning and the bowman must be able to give accurate information about how far off the line you are in order to enable you to be in the front row without being premature.

The two positioning criteria which are important are:

a) There must not be a super high-pointing yacht immediately to leeward. If there was, then she could squeeze you out and force you to tack away or sail in dirty wind.

b) There must not be a really fast, large boat immediately to windward or it will sail over you and soon force you to tack.

These additional complications mean that it is vital to attempt at least to control who is starting around you. If there is a high-pointing yacht to leeward then you must ensure that there is a large enough gap between you so that you are not squeezed out.

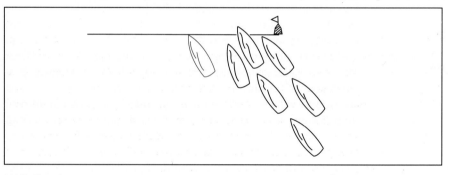

123 Starboard bias - port side of beat

It is possible to achieve this because you will almost certainly have luffing rights over the yacht immediately to windward and can thus luff away from the problem to leeward and create a gap. The problem then is one of timing. If you create your gap too early or too obviously then either another yacht can sail into it, thus creating another problem, or the boat to leeward will just luff and stay close to you. In the former case you can protect the gap by looking behind and being aware of other yachts who are trying to find a gap. If it looks as if there is such a yacht coming in, then a sharp bear away will visually fill the gap and may dissuade the newcomer.

124 Make and keep your gap

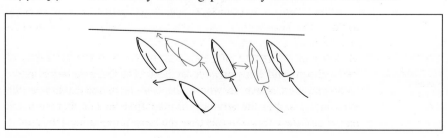

In bearing away like this the tendency will be to accelerate and you must decide - before you actually bear away whether there is enough room to allow acceleration or if the trimmers should stall or ease the sails to slow you down.

Conversely, if there is a large and fast yacht coming in to windward then you should try to squeeze her out before the start. Either force her up such that she starts prematurely or, better still, get your own boat into the 'safe leebow' position so that boat to windward is in your back wind and is herself forced to tack away. Even yachts of quite different sizes affect each other enough for this to be effective, if the manoeuvre is executed properly.

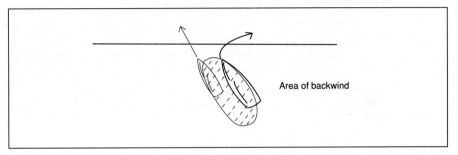

Area of backwind

125 Safe leebow position

There is always a danger in forcing someone else up so that they start prematurely. This is that regardless of whether your judgement of the position of the line is correct or not, you cannot be certain that the yacht will be recalled by the committee and even if she is, circumstances may force her to carry on for long enough to give you dirty wind and leave you buried. This means that you need to be very sure of yourself before trying to force someone over the line and it is normally safer to try to get them where you have real control.

Port-end starts

Port-end starting presents a different range of problems to those experienced when wanting to start at the starboard end of the line. Being early is far more of a problem because it is obviously not possible to carry on a little further down the line on starboard tack. In most cases it is safest to start on starboard tack to ensure at least most of your rights, although you may well not want to get locked into a position too early.

Once again the overall tactics will be dictated by the strategy for the first beat with a split depending on whether it is thought best to head to the right or to the left.

a) Port end - port side of beat: In most ways this is the easier of the two options. Once again the important thing is to be in the front row with clear air and no one about to squeeze you out. Wanting to sail to the left side of the course means that starboard tack is advantageous thus there is no merit in attempting a dangerous port-tack start. The only real problem comes when the line is very heavily biased so that it is really important to start not only in the front row but also as near the pin end as possible. Obviously there is only one yacht which can have clear air and be at the pin and the difficulty lies in trying to find a gap to slot into which will get you as near to this position as possible.

There are basically two ways of finding your position. The first is to approach from behind the line on starboard and reach down behind the row of boats which will be stacked along the line, when you see a suitable gap and nudge your way in, gently persuading the yacht to windward to move up in order to let you into the gap thus formed. The problem with this is that once in a position between other yachts, you have little say in how fast you progress down the line, since the yacht to leeward can slow you down as much as she likes. This can make it very difficult to judge the best gap to get into, especially if you are lining up fairly early.

126 Port end - difficult to find a gap

The other extreme occurs when you decide to try to find a gap but leave it a bit late. Because most of the fleet will be reaching down the line on starboard, the speed difference between the front row and a yacht coming from behind will be small. It will therefore be difficult to find a hole to choose, since the holes will be travelling away from you almost as fast as you are going yourself. What this usually means is that the latecomer has little choice and is forced to take advantage of any gap which is available, even if this is not in an ideal position (see diagram 127).

The one time when this method of approach does work well is when the yacht approaching from behind the front row on starboard is much bigger or faster than the majority of the fleet.

During one memorable series at La Trinite sur Mer in Brittany, I was sailing on a Frers 50-Footer called *Aida* in a Channel Handicap fleet. We were easily the fastest yacht and in fact about half the fleet were 30ft one-design yachts. This meant that we were always able to come from behind with plenty of speed, reach along behind the little yachts until we found the right gap and then surge into it. We never had any problems with dirty wind because our mast and sails were clear of the smaller yachts' sails and we always had enough speed to reach the ideal position since we were so large. This made starting relatively simple, as long as we did not try to 'mix it' too much with the little yachts who were obviously much more manoeuvrable.

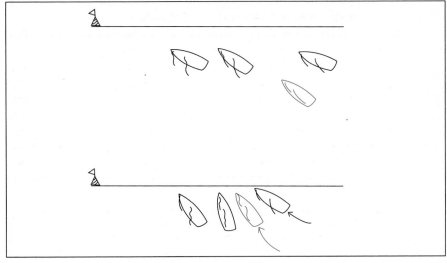

127 Port end - timing affected by other yachts

The alternative method of approaching a port-end start is to come in on port tack - keeping just to leeward of the inevitable row of starboard tackers and keeping a very good lookout. Take your time as the pin end is passed and then keep track of how long you have been going away from it towards the starboard end of the line. Because you will be travelling against the flow, any gaps in the row of starboard tackers will come up quickly and it should be possible to choose one which is suitable both in positional terms and in the context of which yachts will be on either side of your own.

The only real danger with this approach is that if the line is very biased to port, there may be so much bunching that there is no real gap into which to slot. If this is realized early on then it may be best to tack to leeward of the bunch and slow the whole row down by luffing and letting your sails flap.

128 Port end - timed run into a gap

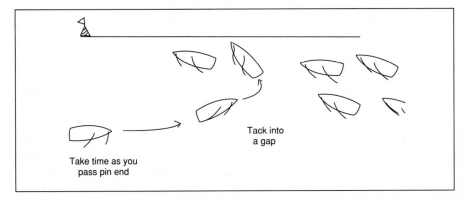

Tack into a gap

Take time as you pass pin end

b) Port end - right side of beat. In this case a compromise will almost certainly have to be made. The ideal way to start would be at the pin on port tack. This is occasionally possible if there is a long line and a lot of port bias, the rest of the fleet have not realized how much bias there is, no starboard tackers are early at the port end and you have a bit of luck.

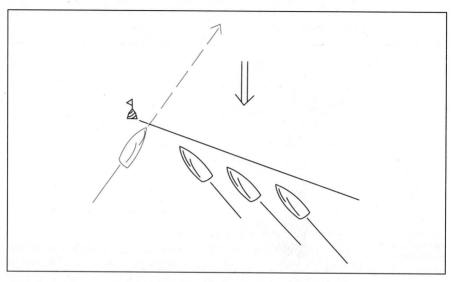

129 Port end - perfect start

A port-tack, pin-end start is, however, usually fraught with danger and should not be undertaken lightly.

This leaves two other options. The first and safest will be to start on starboard tack, giving up a little of the line bias in order to be to windward of a bunch of yachts and hopefully have a large enough gap to tack into soon after the start.

130 Port bias - starboard side of beat: option 1

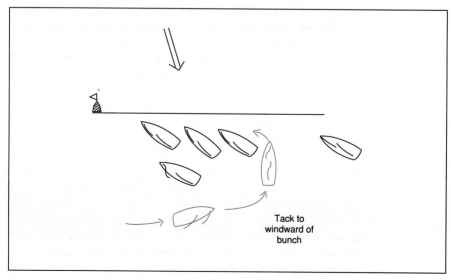

Tack to windward of bunch

The other option is to approach the line on port tack, once again dipping behind the front row starboard tackers as you go. This leaves the option of either tacking into a hole if a suitable one becomes available and it is obvious that a port-tack start is impossible, or ducking a few transoms and continuing on port tack if this looks like the best option at the time. The advantage is that the decision need not be made until very near the start time, thus giving more real choice.

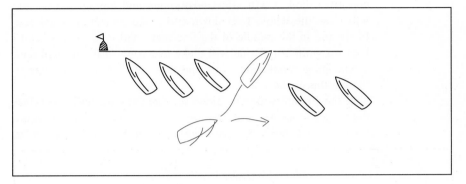

131 Port bias - starboard side of beat: option 2

Starting · the general principles

All the preceding detail about the rules which are applicable and how to consider starting at each end of the line are to no avail unless some general principles are adhered to.

a) Transits: The bowman and tactician must know where the line is at all times. If starting in the middle of the line this becomes even more important since the sag or bulge in the line will increase away from the ends. In the pre-start, therefore, some time should be spent looking along the line from just outside both ends in order to obtain good transits with the shore if this is possible. The navigator should take and check the bearing of the line so that if only one end and no transit can be seen at the start, he can at least check the bearing as a position indicator.

b) Distance to the line: Following on from (a), the bowman should be able to give distance to the line (normally in boat lengths). This should always be expressed in the perpendicular distance from the line with no allowance made for tidal stream or wind angle. The navigator and tactician should be aware of these latter complications and make due allowance for them.

c) Acceleration time and speed: Each yacht will have its own characteristics of acceleration in a particular wind strength. The tactician must know how his yacht will respond in order to be able to judge when to turn the speed on or off in the final approach to the line. Similarly, at maximum speed the yacht will take a certain number of seconds to travel one boat length - this must also be in the back of the tactician's mind while watching the bowman call the distance to the line.

d) Intimidation: For the less experienced, a crowded start line can be a very intimidating situation. The only remedy is to practise starting until you are no longer frightened by it and have a good enough knowledge of the size and performance of the yacht to be able to control the start to your advantage.

e) Tidal streams: Be aware of the direction and strength of any tidal stream at the line. The navigator needs to worry about how this will affect the strategy, but the tactician needs to be concerned how it will affect positioning and timing. A foul tide will slow the whole fleet down and make premature starts less likely and in the middle of the line there will tend to be a sag to leeward while a fair tide will make everyone early and will tend to encourage premature starts and there will often be a bulge in the middle of the line.

If the stream is running along the line then this will also affect the tactics at the start. If the tide is taking yachts away from the favoured end this will often open up a gap for the aware person

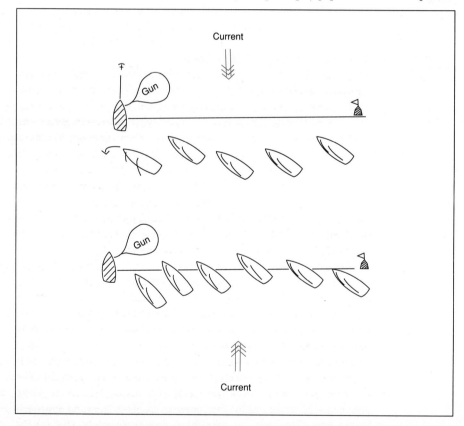

132 Effect of current

just at the start, whereas if the tide is taking the fleet onto the favoured end then you know there will be extra bunching and no gap.

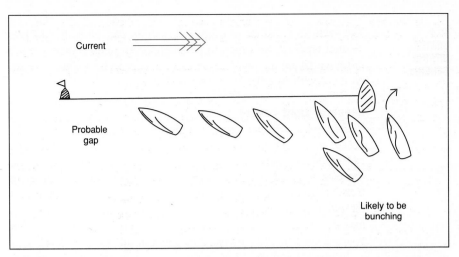

Current

Probable
gap

Likely to be
bunching

133 Effect of
current along
the line

f) Premature starting: Some committees will signal a general recall at the drop of a hat, others hesitate to recall even one yacht unless the premature start is really blatant. It is valuable to know which sort of committee is running the race so that your tactics can be altered to suit.

Starting at the committee-boat end will always leave you vulnerable to recall because you are the yacht which is seen. Similarly, popping out of the middle of a bunch of boats with really good boat speed and a prominently coloured bow makes it easy for the committee to decide that you were premature.

Be aware of the bowman's call if he thinks you were early and get used to trusting him - otherwise there is little point in him being there at all. Once you are sure that a premature start has been made - and noticed - bite the bullet and restart as quickly as possible. If the committee are going to read out recall numbers on the radio, then make sure someone is listening if there is any possibility of your being recalled.

During one of the inshore races on *Wings of Oracle* in the 1991 Admiral's Cup, we had a brilliant start but our skipper believed we were over the line and returned before any recall numbers had been announced. Due to unfortunate circumstances, we had a new bowman for that day who had never sailed with us before and although he said that we were OK, there was not enough trust to believe him fully. This lost us the start and ultimately the race. My advice when recall numbers are being used would be to wait until you are recalled before returning. If you were noticed then a return will put you into last place whether done sooner or later, but if you have got away with a slightly early start then why give up the advantage unless forced? Only go back before being told to do so if there has been an individual recall signal and you *know* that it must be for your yacht.

**10.4
BEATING
UPWIND –
GENERAL**

The tactics of sailing upwind successfully can be split into two distinct types: those which force an opponent to do something and those which are merely defensive. Most boat-to-boat situations can be dealt with in either way as we shall see.

Loose or tight cover?

Regardless of whether you are on port or starboard tack, if you are ahead in a crossing situation you have three basic choices. You can ignore the opposition and continue on your own way or you can tack in one of two ways. In the latter case you may decide to tack into such a position that your dirty wind or back wind affects the other yacht and forces him to tack away (tight cover) or you may decide to tack so that you are between him and the mark but you are not actually slowing him down at all (loose cover).

In general you would put tight cover on an opponent when you want to force him to go the other way. This is a form of active 'shepherding', useful when there is a definite right way to go. I would also tend to use this form of cover when I was concerned that the performance of our yacht was not sufficient to be safe in a straight fight between us and the particular competitor, thus relying on better strategy to beat him.

Loose cover is used when the strategy is less certain and you just want to stay between your opponent and the next mark. This is useful especially if you feel confident that in a fair match you would have the advantage, thus reducing the point of trying to force your opposition away. In offshore races having a competitor breathing metaphorically down your neck will also spur you on to sail faster and will tend to heighten the performance of both yachts.

Port tacker meets starboard tacker

134 Port tack
gives way to
starboard

Everyone knows (hopefully) that a port tack yacht must give way to one on starboard tack, but there are many ways of fulfilling that obligation.

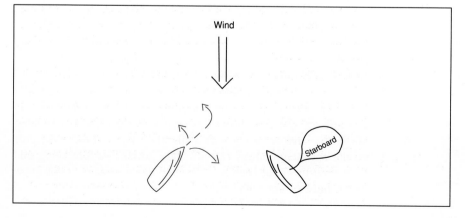

a) <u>Port-tack yacht wants to carry on and is just ahead:</u> In this situation, the port-tack yacht wants to stay on port tack for strategic reasons and is just far enough ahead to warrant the risk of passing in front of the starboard tacker.

A good watch needs to be kept on the starboard tacker to check for a steady bearing and if the supposition that it was possible to sail ahead of the starboard tacker was correct, then all is well. Make sure that the starboard tacker knows you are there by hailing 'hold your course' or words to that effect. It is not that this hail is binding but simply that you don't want a sudden panic on the part of the starboard tacker if he only realizes your presence very late. Continue watching him until you are completely clear, because this is a very vulnerable position.

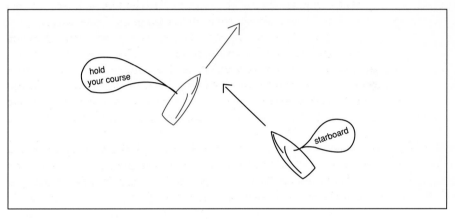

135 Port tack
crossing ahead

As a general rule in any potential port and starboard collision situation, the starboard tacker will be assumed to be in the right unless the port tacker can *prove* that there was no need for him to alter course.

The real problem with trying to pass ahead in a marginal situation is not so much the danger of collision or protest, but more the danger of realizing late on in the situation that you have made a mistake and will not after all be able to cross ahead. In this case you will be forced to tack, thus going 'the wrong way' and often the tack will be poorly executed because it will inevitably be a last-minute affair.

b) <u>Port tacker wants to carry on and cannot cross ahead:</u> Here the port tacker wants once again to stay on port tack for strategic gain but is too close to risk crossing ahead of the starboard tacker. In this case ducking behind the starboard tacker in an organized way is the best solution and should lose little, if any, ground.

Try to decide on the plan as soon as possible to allow for a neat bear away around the starboard tacker's transom rather than a last-minute panic manoeuvre. In this way the sails can be eased a touch with a corresponding increase in boat speed and the optimum course can be sailed so that your yacht is heading in the right direction as the other yacht flashes past.

There will be a significant lift as the starboard tacker goes past and his back wind is experienced. If the port tacker is close enough to him and able to luff up as soon as his transom has cleared then it should be possible to come out of a ducking manoeuvre approximately level with the starboard yacht. If, on the other hand, the manoeuvre is left until too late then the port tacker will be facing the wrong way with her sails stalled as the starboard tacker goes past and will lose at least one or two boat lengths.

136 Port tack ducking behind - efficiently

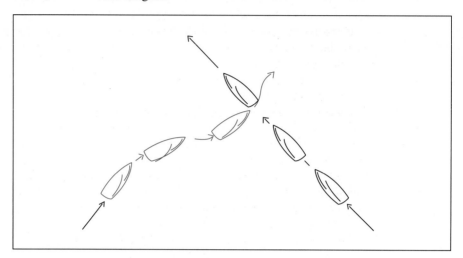

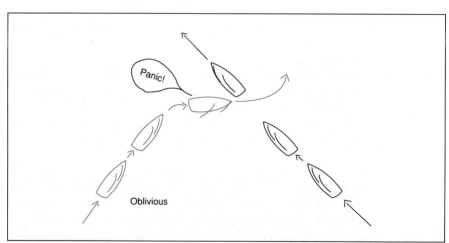

137 Inefficient ducking manoeuvre

<u>c) Port tacker wants to tack onto starboard for strategic gain:</u> In this case the plan will be to tack onto starboard so close to the competitor that she is forced to tack away; the manoeuvre is called 'the leebow tack' (see diagram 138).

To execute a successful leebow tack it is important that the two yachts are at least of comparable size and speed. I once made the mistake of trying to leebow an 80ft maxi from a 53ft Swan and although the manoeuvre was completed to perfection the maxi still just sailed straight over us - furthermore, in the next race the situation was reversed and having a maxi leebow you is not an experience you want repeated!

The other criterion for the manoeuvre to have a chance of being successful is that the port tacker needs to be at least half a boat length ahead before the start of the manoeuvre, otherwise the starboard tacker will almost certainly have the boat speed to sail over the top of the newly tacked yacht.

If the above criteria are satisfied then the leebow manoeuvre itself should go as follows:

i) Make certain that the starboard tack yacht knows not only that you are there but also that you are taking action to avoid him (to avoid a possible protest).

ii) Sail on the low side of the 'groove' as you approach so as to build up good speed - crack sheets a tiny bit if necessary.

iii) Brief your crew that a leebow tack is about to happen - the tack must be a good one!

iv) Tack as late as possible consistent with not tacking in his water. This means that he must not need to start altering course to keep clear of you until you have completed your tack - that is until you have borne away to a close-hauled course.

v) After the tack do not try to squeeze up immediately. Sail slightly low to start with and accelerate to your optimum speed before starting slowly to wind in the sheets and point higher. If you attempt to sail high straight after the tack, the manoeuvre will almost certainly fail.

vi) Once you have matched the speed of you opponent, it is possible to give him real dirty wind by oversheeting the mainsail slightly, not too much or you will be slowed down, just enough to get the top tell tale stalled out.

vii) At this stage he will either sag into your dirty wind and eventually drop behind or will tack away (see diagram 138).

<u>d) Port tacker wants to tack onto starboard and also wants starboard tacker to come with him:</u> The time that this is the correct tactic is when you realize that it will be advantageous to tack onto starboard and you want to cover an opponent. Either you are just ahead and want to stay between him and the next mark or you are not sure about which the favoured side will be and therefore do not want to risk forcing him away to his possible advantage.

This is where an early tack onto starboard is called for, tacking to leeward of the starboard tacker so that your dirty wind does not affect him and you are not posing an immediate threat.

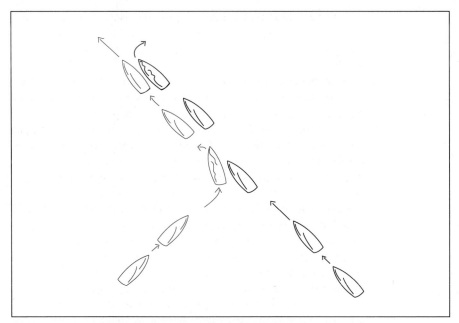

138 Leebow
tack

Starboard tacker meets port tacker

Over the next few paragraphs we will consider the same boat-to-boat situations as looked at above, but this time from the point of view of the starboard-tack yacht.

a) Starboard tacker wants to stay on this tack: Here the object of the exercise will be to prevent the port-tack yacht from effectively executing a leebow manoeuvre. There are two ways to proceed, one 'passively' and the other with aggression. The passive way will be to wave the port tacker on and hope that he takes the offer.

There is a problem here, though: it is not actually possible to wave away your rights in this manner and it is akin to flashing your lights at another car while driving. You could probably be held to be sailing unfairly if a collision happened but in any case the port-tack yacht is under no obligation to obey your request for him to continue sailing. If you have waved him on it is likely that you will have had to bear away slightly to pass around his stern and this will obviously have put you into a less advantageous position if he decides to try a leebow tack.

I would recommend that this approach is only taken when the port tacker is almost clear ahead anyway and you are therefore losing nothing by waving him through. If the two boats are more or less level and similar in size then careful positive action should prevent most leebow tacks from being effective.

The best way actively to prevent a leebow tack from being effective is to make the port tacker go about too early so that there is good separation after the tack. Once you have seen the port tacker and realize that a leebow tack may be his intention, sail a little bit low and fast in order to bring you together a little further to leeward than otherwise. If he starts to duck you or tacks early then you can immediately go back to normal target speed and height.

If, on the other hand, he gets close enough to cause you problems after the tack then as soon as he commences his tack you should sail really high for a while, until you have burnt off the excess speed which you had from sailing low. This in itself should give you at least a boat length of separation which will probably keep you out of your opponent's back wind. Once down to normal target speed it will be important to sail normally and not pinch too much. This technique should give you the best chance of staying on starboard tack but sometimes he will still get you in his back wind. In general terms, as soon as you recognize that he is going to squeeze you out you should immediately tack away, since in most cases two tacks with good speed will lose you much less than allowing yourself to be slowed down before eventually admitting defeat anyway.

b) Starboard tacker wants to tack to port: This puts the starboard tack yacht into a slightly difficult position. She is 'the right of way yacht' and rule 35 prevents her from altering course in such a way 'as to prevent the other yacht from keeping clear or so as to obstruct her while she is keeping clear'. In most cases this effectively rules out a leebow tack except in situations where the port-tack yacht is not attempting to keep clear.

An alternative which has been deemed to be allowed is the 'slam dunk'. Here, the starboard tack yacht goes just past the port tacker and then tacks to windward of her so as to give her dirty air and thus force her to tack. Great care needs to be taken, because rule 41 gives rights to the port tack yacht who is 'on a tack' rather than to the tacking yacht. In effect there must be space for you to complete your tack before the port tacker has to start taking any further avoiding action.

139 Slam dunk by starboard tacker

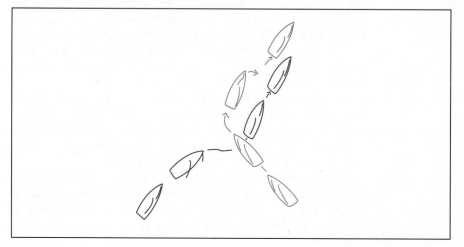

Dealing with obstructions

An obstruction is defined in the Yacht Racing Rules as 'any object including a vessel under way, large enough to require a yacht, when more than one overall length away from it to make a substantial alteration of course to pass on one side or the other, or any object that can be passed safely on one side only, including a buoy when the yacht in question cannot safely pass between it and the shoal or object which it marks'.

Most of the rules which deal with obstructions are also those which are used for mark rounding and more specific detail will be included later in the chapter.

The majority of sailors manage to deal with most obstructions with no real problems as the rules covering how and when water needs to be given are fairly clear. It is the '. . . including a vessel under way' bit of the definition which seems to give most problems. This part of the definition means that if the leeward of two port tackers wants to tack to get out of the way of a starboard tacker, it is perfectly legitimate for her to call for water to tack and the windward yacht must respond, even if he would have preferred to duck behind the starboard tacker or if he could otherwise have passed ahead of her.

140 Water to tack for a starboard tacker

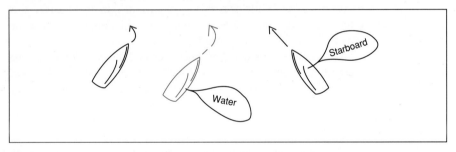

In a situation when both port tackers decide to pass behind the starboard tacker, then normal rules for claiming water apply and in general terms the inside yacht will need to be given room. The details of when water must be given are contained in rule 42.

141 Calling for 'water' for a starboard tacker

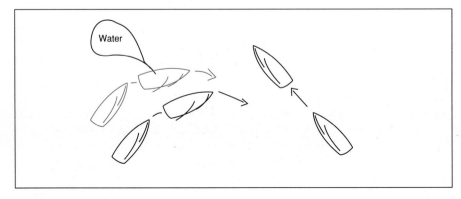

Think ahead when tacking

In nearly every case, each tack will slow you down a little and, more important still, a second tack before your speed has recovered from the first tack will lose you large amounts of ground. These facts, obvious though they are, mean that you must think carefully about your position and that of the other yachts in your fleet before each tack.

The cone of dirty, turbulent air from a yacht's sails extends downwind for up to about eight times the mast height - maybe 10 boat lengths. The effect will obviously be less as you get further away and will not be so great on a day when the wind is gusty and turbulent anyway but it always amazes me just how far this zone of interference does extend. The back wind from the sails is more localized, extending about one boat length to windward and one or two boat lengths behind.

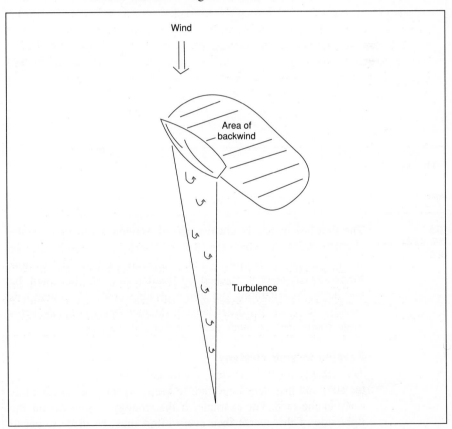

142 Dirty air

When tacking you need to be on the look out for other yachts which may be about to tack as well so that you are not forced to tack again too soon. You should also think about the relative losses of staying in someone's dirt compared to putting in yet another one or two tacks. It sometimes pays to hang in and ignore the turbulence if it is not too bad.

When tacking to leeward of a competitor you can sometimes use him as a barrier to prevent other yachts tacking on top of you by tacking so that you are only just out of the first yacht's dirt, thus giving no room for anyone else to get between you.

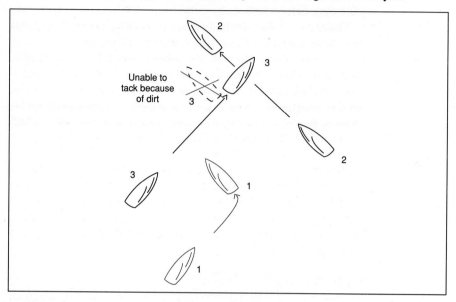

Unable to tack because of dirt

143 Use starboard tacker to keep your air clean

10.5 THE FIRST BEAT

The first beat is nearly always critical. Having got away from the starting line this is where the fleet is closest together and therefore where there are most opportunities for positive tactics. By the time the windward mark is reached for the first time, the fleet will, by and large, be separating out into a pecking order. Of course it is possible to upset this order later in the race but it certainly helps to go round the top mark near the front of the fleet.

Keeping to your strategy

The strategy for this first leg should have been worked out before the start and it is very important to keep to your plan, at least this early in the race. For example, if the strategy was to favour the right side of the course then every effort must be made to get to that side as soon as possible after the start.

Only consider throwing away your initial game plan if it is obviously not paying and you can appreciate why another plan would work better. In particular, do not allow yourselves to be panicked into abandoning a perfectly good plan just because of short-term gains being made by other yachts. The first few miles of the 1991 Fastnet illustrates a very good example of how sticking to your guns can pay off, even if it is hard in the short term.

On *Wings of Oracle*, we had discussed before the start whether to go to the left of the beat down the Solent, which is where most of the fleet would be short tacking, or to the right, onto the mainland shore where there would be a starboard lift, good tide and much less interference from other yachts. The difficulty was that the immediate gains were to be had to the left.

In the event our start, in the middle of the line in foul tide, meant that we had little choice but to go to the right and we did this with only one other Admiral's Cup yacht for company. As per the pre-race discussion, the rest of the fleet gained during the opening minutes of the race and as navigator I was under tremendous pressure from the crew to 'give in' and allow us to rejoin the fleet on the left side of the course.

However, we held onto our right-hand berth and eventually, when the tidal conditions had evened out over the whole course joined the remainder of the fleet - ahead of all our competition. Had we given up even five minutes earlier then we would have been at the back of our fleet, thus showing that a properly reasoned plan will often pay.

Watch the fleet

Even if your plan looks secure, it is important to keep track on how the rest of the fleet are faring. I like to note a few close competitors and take bearings on them as often as necessary to ascertain who is doing best.

If by the second half of the beat it becomes obvious that another strategy is called for and that your competitors are doing consistently better in another place, then there comes a time when you must bite the bullet and join them. This is nearly always a very hard decision because it is rare to be able to get across to the other side of a beat without losing ground in the process and it is often tempting to hang on and on, hoping for some magic to happen until you are eventually forced to realize your mistake. As stated previously, do ensure that you are not merely panicking about a short-term situation which is about to change in your favour.

No duels yet

At this early stage in the race it is vital that you sail your own race as far as possible and do not get drawn into boat-for-boat duels with any single competitors.

Even when thinking about a tack in a situation where the choice is between tacking so as to affect a competitor or tacking into a loose cover sort of position, it can sometimes pay to appear magnanimous and take the latter course in order to avoid a grudge being held against you for later in the race.

The only occasion when it is worth getting into tacking duels or otherwise attempting to slow down one particular competitor is when the race is the last in a series and you only need to beat this one yacht in order to improve your overall position.

10.6 **THE FINAL** **BEAT**	The final beat can also be treated somewhat differently to the rest of the race. In general your tactics should be to conserve whatever position you have achieved by the last leeward mark while also attacking the yacht directly ahead of you. Psychologically it is far worse to lose places near the finish than at any other time, whereas a place gained in the last few minutes of a race is sweet indeed.

Tacking duels

The final leg is the time for one-to-one matches, either defensively against a competitor who is attacking from close behind or aggressively against a yacht in a catchable position ahead. This assumes that there is no risk of losing more places in a handicap fleet by 'wasting' more time than you stand to gain.

Tacking duels start when you get close enough to the yacht ahead to make him need to cover you. If you then tack away from him he is more or less forced to follow your lead in case you get a better shift or whatever, as soon as he has tacked you then tack again and so on. The yacht ahead should win most duels but the final outcome will ultimately be decided by the crew which makes fewest mistakes.

Tactically, you should try to tack on any little shift that is in your favour, since you will be tacking just before your opponent this may give you a slight advantage.

If you are the tactician of the leading yacht in a duel like this, try not to be forced to tack too often into an unfavourable position and if the yachts are really close attempt to stay just to starboard of your competitor so that in the event of an opposite tacks collision situation, you will always be on starboard with the right of way.

Loose cover, unless threatened

If you are ahead of a close competitor, it is usually better to use loose cover while going up the final beat in order to encourage him to go the same way as yourself. Once you put tight cover on an opponent, that will inevitably force him to tack away, which will probably force you to tack to cover, and so a tacking duel has been started!

Only start using tight cover when the yacht behind is threatening to get past you and you therefore need to take active steps to prevent being overtaken.

Conservative tactics and strategy, unless behind

As a general rule the final beat is the time for conservative sailing, both from the tactical and strategic points of view. If you have spent the whole race working yourselves into a reasonable or good position, then this is not the time to throw all that work away with a flier or by having to take a penalty after any unnecessary boat-to-boat situations.

If, on the other hand, the position you find yourself in at the start of the final beat is not satisfactory, then maybe this is the right time to make a last-ditch attempt to improve - realizing that taking a risk may worsen your position even further.

**10.7
THE
WINDWARD
MARK**

Reaching the layline and rounding the top mark are nearly always tricky situations, especially if the fleet is large or closely matched. The majority of sensible race officers will give a port-mark rounding at least for the first mark so that yachts on the easy, starboard layline, have right of way - but not all race officers will do this, so beware. As with other parts of the beat, it is important to plan your approach to the mark rather than just somehow arriving there with little control over the situation.

Port rounding, starboard layline

Once you are on the layline your options from both a tactical and strategic point of view are strictly limited. You will be unable to make use of wind shifts and will also not be able to do much to control your position in relation to your competitors. This means that getting onto the starboard layline very early is normally a mistake. On the other hand, getting onto the layline very late has its own problems from both tactical and crew work points of view.

If you decide or are forced for whatever reason to be on the layline relatively early, compared with the majority of the fleet, then in most situations you should leave yourself a little room in hand to allow for other yachts tacking on your line and thus making it more difficult to lay the buoy. However, it is obviously not good to overdo this since any overstanding of the mark is effectively distance lost. If the tidal stream is sweeping you up to the mark then it may be best to understand a little since it will be fairly easy to squeeze up a little and make it around the buoy.

If another yacht is approaching the layline a little way either ahead or behind you, it can pay to attempt to confuse them as to whether you are on the best layline or not. If you have overstood the mark, it would be best to get the other yacht to sail even further past the buoy than you because, even in dirt it should not be a problem for you to lay it. You can sometimes do this by deliberately aiming a bit below the buoy as your opponent approaches; he can often be fooled by this. Then as soon as he has gone past your line, you should point up again.

In the opposite situation, when you are really struggling to lay the buoy or you already know that you are just not quite going to make it, the best plan will be to get the other yacht to tack under your line, thus forcing him to put in two extra tacks. In this case, get good speed up as he is approaching and then point the yacht so that it looks as if you are making the buoy easily as he gets more or less to your line.

144 Laying the mark - persuade the opposition to overstand

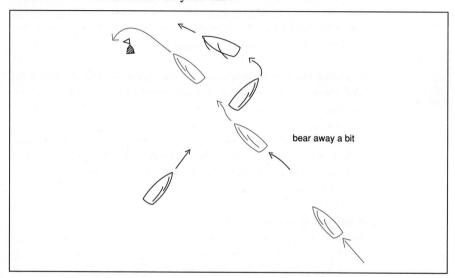

bear away a bit

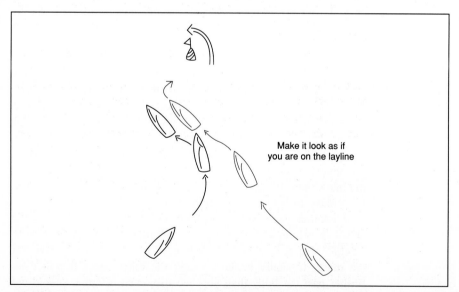

Make it look as if you are on the layline

145 Not laying the mark - persuade the opposition to tack early

If you are approaching the starboard layline and there are already yachts on the layline then you must decide whether to tack beneath them or to sail beyond their line. This is a very difficult judgement call and one where, as we have seen, the opposition will be doing their best to confuse you. Going past the line of other yachts will lose you some ground if they were right on the layline but tacking too early and having to try to put two more tacks in very near the mark will undoubtedly lose you far more. If in doubt, it is usually safer to overstand rather than understand the mark.

Port rounding, port layline

Arriving either on the port layline itself or even just late onto the starboard layline with a port rounding coming up gives everyone on the yacht some problems. It will obviously be more difficult for the crew to set up for the mark rounding since a tack set will be called for and therefore the pole will not be able to be raised until the actual rounding, and so on. From a tactical point of view, the difficulty will lie in finding the best gap into which to tack - or possibly in finding a gap at all.

One point which must always be remembered if on the port layline is that the rules for claiming water at a mark *do not apply* to yachts on opposite tacks when beating. Rule 42.b specifically excludes this from its normal provisions.

If the fleet is closely bunched at this stage of the race, then the starboard layline may well be very crowded and finding a gap to slot into can take some contriving. If there is a smaller or much slower boat already on the layline then it may be possible to tack to leeward of her and then point high and thus make a gap to squeeze into. Similarly, if the boats on starboard have overstood the line then it should be possible to tack to leeward of them and still lay the mark.

The rules allow a port tacker to tack to leeward of a starboard tacker within two boat lengths of the buoy and still call for water. This is because a new overlap will have been established as soon as the tack is complete. The inside yacht is then allowed to luff as far as head to wind in order to get round the buoy but may not tack, so the decision on whether to tack to leeward is quite critical.

If the tide is setting you onto the mark once the tack onto starboard has been completed this is an extremely risky situation, since it is unlikely that the yachts already on the layline will have overstood by much.

During the 1987 Admiral's Cup, I watched in horror as *Jamarella*, one of the British team, tacked into an ever-decreasing gap at the top mark. She tacked immediately to leeward of one of the German team and had to luff all the way as far as head to wind in order to shoot the buoy. The German yacht was unable to respond to the luff and the situation ended with both yachts being wedged firmly onto the buoy with other yachts sailing around the pair. In the ensuing protest, *Jamarella* was exonerated with the help of some excellent photographic evidence but the manoeuvre had still cost her several places. Even at that level it is often difficult to judge if a tack to leeward of the fleet is safe or not.

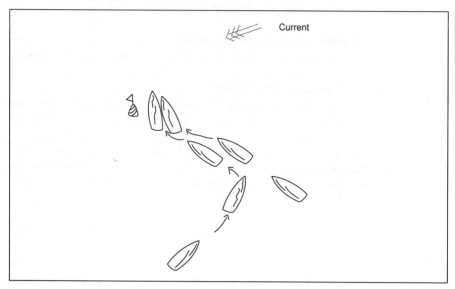
Current

146 The danger of under estimating the current

On another occasion, I was sailing in a club race and we approached the windward mark on the port layline, but this time the tide was setting starboard tackers away from the buoy rather than onto it.

Although the row of boats on the starboard layline all looked as if they were only just making the buoy, we decided that with the tidal direction it must be possible to squeeze in and in fact did so successfully. Had we tried to find a gap to sail into, we would have had to duck at least three or four yachts and would probably never have made up those places later in the race.

If you look at the situation and realize that there is no way that tacking to leeward is going to be successful, then you must bail out as early as possible. If there is no gap at the buoy itself then the only realistic option is to bear off and sail parallel to the starboard layline until a gap appears, then tack into the gap.

147 Port layline can be expensive

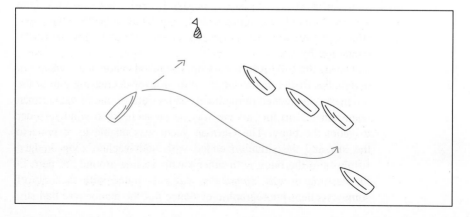

Whichever option you chose make sure that the crew realize what is happening, otherwise a difficult situation will undoubtedly turn into an impossible one.

Starboard rounding, port layline

If this situation occurs anywhere near the start of a closely fought race then, in my opinion, the race committee have not been sensible. The problem with a starboard, windward mark rounding is that yachts which approach the buoy on the otherwise simpler port layline, so that they can get their spinnaker gear set, etc., will have no rights at all over yachts arriving at the layline later on starboard and this invariably ends in frustration for someone.

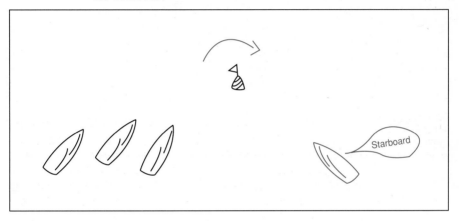

148 Starboard rounding

If you do have to approach the buoy from the port layline it is important to keep a close watch for any starboard tackers who may cause you problems. If you foresee a potential collision situation your only real options are either to duck the starboard tacker in good time, or be forced about.

When deciding whether to duck or tack, the main consideration should be whether or not you were easily fetching the buoy before the alteration was required. If you had overstood, then a duck behind the starboard tacker should not lose too much ground and, if lucky, you might even be able to stay ahead of her. If, on the other hand, you were struggling to lay the buoy in any case, a duck behind another yacht will almost certainly mean that you would not lay the mark afterwards.

In this case I would duck if the starboard tacker was nearly clear ahead because when you then come back on starboard tack it is likely that you would have the advantage. If it was a touch-and-go situation with you almost being able to pass ahead of the starboard tacker, it is probably better to tack under his leebow, force him to tack as soon as possible and then tack again yourself (see diagrams 149 – 150).

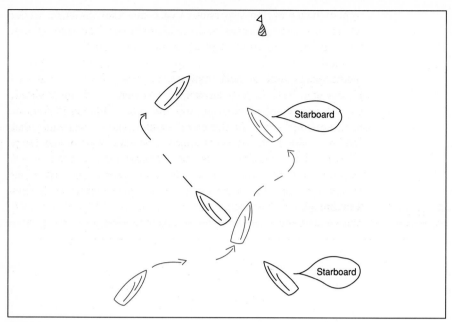

149 Starboard rounding - get inside

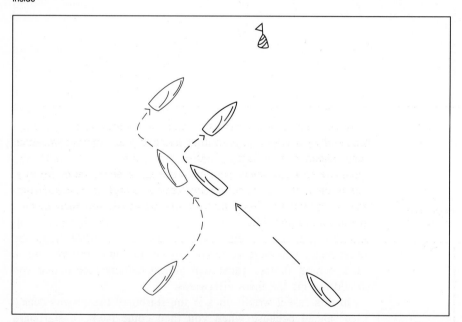

150 Tack if you are nearly ahead

Starboard rounding, starboard layline

In this case you have most of the cards, certainly as far as the right of way is concerned, but not all of them.

Any yachts which have arrived at the mark on port tack will obviously have to give way and if you are really on the starboard layline then the chief worry will be other yachts tacking under your leebow and possibly giving you dirty air. The leebow tack situation has been covered in detail in section 10.4.

Another possible problem is being followed into the mark with another yacht right on your transom, or even a little to windward of your line. Rule 42.2 states quite clearly that a yacht clear ahead, is subject to rule 41 and is not allowed to tack directly in front of the following boat - 'in the other yacht's water'. Assuming that you are in the yacht which is clear ahead then your best defence is a very tight rounding of the mark followed by a quick tack if the situation looks safe. If not, a delayed tack until the following yacht commences her own tack is the only safe alternative. If your crew are all ready and do a better tack followed by a better hoist then you can often find yourself in a commanding position anyway.

151 Luff hard after the buoy

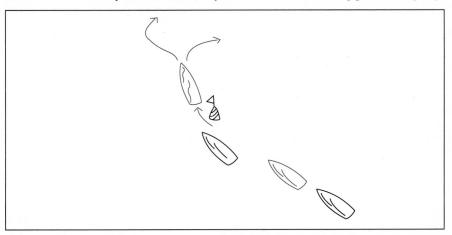

If you are in the following yacht, a slightly wide approach followed by a very tight rounding and sharp luff may prevent the yacht ahead from tacking. If this is the case, then the luff can become a tack and away you go. If the yacht ahead tacks anyway and is clear then it is normally better to continue just past her line, unless the next leg is a run when you should be bearing away as quickly as possible.

152 Prevent the yacht ahead from tacking

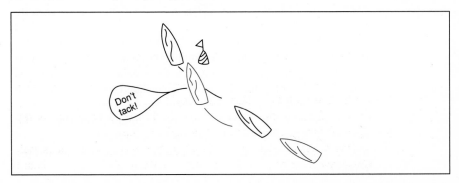

**10.8
REACHING**

The tactics when reaching can be broken into three separate parts: keeping clear air, overtaking situations and getting a tow.

Keeping your air clear

It is very important on a reach to sail in clear air whenever possible. The effect of dirty air cannot be over emphasized, since it can slow you down for the whole leg. In general terms this means that you should not be sailing to leeward of other yachts unless they are either much slower or much faster than your own yacht.

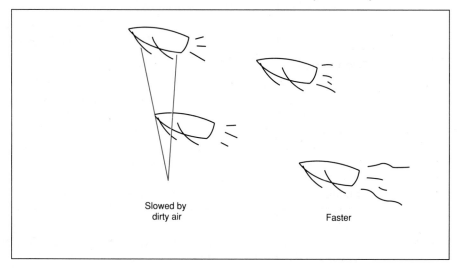

Slowed by
dirty air

Faster

153 Keep your air clear on a reach

There are two real dangers to sailing to leeward of another yacht, one being the slowing effect of the particular boat which is to weather. If she is only a little slower than yourself, the dirt from her may well slow you down enough to stop you from overtaking even over a long period. Even if she is considerably smaller or slower than your yacht, the turbulent air can still slow you down significantly.

The other real danger is that if one yacht is allowed to sit on your wind, this might allow a whole stream of other yachts to overtake you while you are being slowed down. In general terms this means that if one larger and faster yacht is trying to overtake you to weather, especially if she is not in your class, it is no real problem to let her go past. Assuming she is much faster than you, the dirty air will only last for a very short period of time and your losses will be marginal. If, on the other hand, the larger yacht is being followed by other yachts who are in your class and who you would normally expect to be able to hold off on a reach, the danger of allowing the one fast yacht to overtake to weather is that in doing so she may slow you down enough to let all the rest through as well.

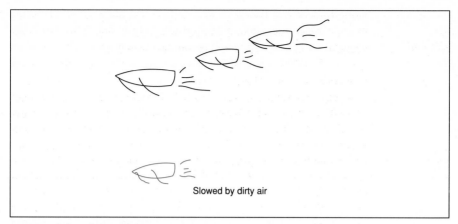

Slowed by dirty air

154 Big yacht helping smaller ones past you

Overtaking

If you are catching up to a yacht ahead, there are two basic ways that you can overtake her on a reach. The easiest by far will be to go to windward of the other yacht so that you are not slowed by her dirty air at all. The problem with this is that the yacht being overtaken is unlikely to want to be passed on the windward side and may try to prevent you from so doing. The alternative in most situations is to aim to pass a long way to leeward in order to minimize the effect of her sails on your wind - at least four or five boat lengths will be required unless she is much smaller than your yacht.

a) Overtaking to windward: If you decide to pass to windward, the earlier this decision is made the better and easier it will be to succeed. A gradual luff to windward from well behind can take you far enough away from the boat ahead so that she will not feel overly threatened by your presence. It will also not slow you down too much nor add significant distance for you to sail.

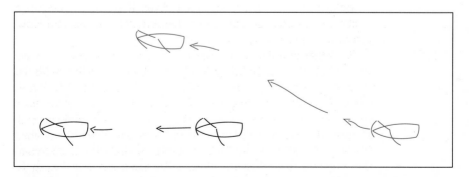

155 Decide early if you want to go to windward

If when you start to luff out to windward of the yacht ahead, he responds and also sails higher, it will be obvious that he is not prepared to let you through to windward and is going to defend his position. In this case you should decide if a luffing match is going to be worth the effort or whether it would after all be better to overtake to leeward. In general a luffing match will slow both yachts involved since you will be sailing much higher than otherwise necessary. If the yacht ahead is of similar size and is determined to stop you, it will be very difficult to break through and could lose quite a lot of time. This is not important in one-design racing as long as no other yachts sneak through to leeward while the luffing is going on, but in a handicap fleet any loss in time may also lose places.

b) Overtaking to leeward: There will be some occasions when you have decided to try to overtake to leeward and the yacht ahead once again attempts to stop you by sailing low himself. The rules allow him to do this until you get within three boat lengths of the other yacht at which time he must revert to sailing his 'proper course'.

While you are still clear astern of the other yacht, he has no obligation to keep clear but as soon as you are overlapped, he must allow you to sail your proper course (rule 39). This rule does not permit luffing on the part of the overtaking yacht unless she was previously sailing below her proper course in order to get to leeward of the yacht ahead. Also, rule 37.3 states that the yacht which has established an overlap from clear astern 'shall initially allow the windward yacht ample room and opportunity to keep clear'.

156 Overtaking to leeward

Being overtaken

Most of the above comments regarding overtaking can be applied in reverse to the overtaken yacht. She must decide whether to allow the following yacht to get into a situation where she is able to overtake to windward. If it is decided to attempt to prevent this then, as implied above, early defensive action needs to be taken to show that your position is not going to be easily given up. If the situation does develop into a luffing match, then any luffs should be vicious and dramatic, a slow shallow luff will only slow both of you down and is unlikely to prevent a faster yacht from overtaking. If you do want to be able to luff then it is important to be on, or at least very near to, the line of the overtaking yacht before commencing a luff or the manoeuvre is doomed to failure.

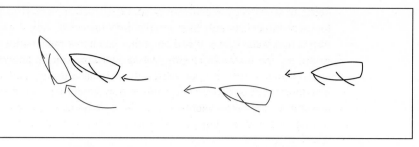

157 Any luff
must be
determined

If the windward yacht has got mast abeam or is obviously going to get through anyway, the leeward yacht should give up the fight and immediately sag off to leeward as far as possible in order to increase the distance between the yachts and so reduce the effects of dirty wind.

One fact which is often used in dinghy racing but which is rarely invoked with yachts is that rule 39.2 allows the leeward yacht to 'luff as she pleases', after the start at least. This means that there is no need to warn the windward yacht of your intention, and if she fails to keep out of your way and for example your spinnaker pole touches her spinnaker, then she would be in the wrong and will be penalized. The danger in taking such a hard line is that it is sometimes difficult to keep really fine control on yachts when luffing and real damage may occur. Quite apart from the undesirability of this anyway, if serious damage is caused then both boats are liable to penalty.

If sailing within the same fleet on a regular basis then a reputation as someone who will luff hard is very useful. Just having once luffed a competitor really hard, regardless of the consequences, is often enough to persuade others not to try to pass to windward.

Taking a tow

In handicap racing, or when more than one class is sharing the same course, there will inevitably be times when larger yachts are overtaking smaller ones. This will give the smaller yachts the opportunity to try to get a 'tow' in the stern wave of the larger yacht as she goes by.

As a general guide, it will be difficult or impossible to get a tow unless the following conditions are met:
a) The larger yacht must be travelling at or near hull speed in order to be dragging a sufficiently large wave to make towing feasible.
b) The speed difference when establishing the tow must not be greater than about one knot unless the smaller yacht is very light and surfs particularly easily.

Tactically, the decision that the yacht trying to get a tow will have to make is whether it will be best to allow the large yacht to pass to windward or to force it to pass to leeward. If the overtaking yacht is much bigger and faster, then it should be forced to go to leeward, since the smaller boat's dirty air will then slow the overtaking yacht down a little and may thus allow the smaller yacht to initiate the tow. Once being towed along, it is quite possible to achieve much greater than usual speeds and so the smaller yacht should then do everything possible not to hinder her benefactor.

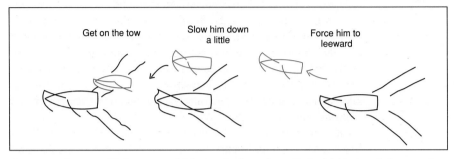

Get on the tow   Slow him down a little   Force him to leeward

158 Getting a tow from a much bigger yacht

If the overtaking yacht is only a little bigger and faster, then forcing her to go to leeward may well stop her from overtaking at all, so in this case she should be allowed to overtake to windward. The smaller yacht should stay quite well to leeward until she experiences dirty air and she should then luff really hard to get through the dirt as quickly as possible and get onto the windward yacht's primary stern wave.

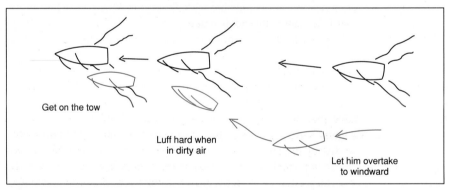

Get on the tow

Luff hard when in dirty air

Let him overtake to windward

159 Getting a tow from a similar-sized yacht

A tow can be a huge advantage and really does not slow down the towing yacht at all.

In one race I was steering a Three-Quarter-Tonner and we got a tow from a Swan 51 which we kept for over 20 miles. This took us slowly but surely into a position some four miles ahead of the next yacht in our class!. On another occasion a J-24 got onto the stern wave of the 53-footer where I was tactician and she stayed there for about 20 minutes, hanging on to our stern wave and feeling really good. However, the conditions changed after about the first five minutes such that other J-24s were actually faster than us and I am convinced that our stern wave actually slowed the J-24 down.

The other times when a tow is not such a good idea, even if the towing yacht is definitely faster, is when she is not going the right way.

During the 1991 Fastnet, we reached the rock in *Wings of Oracle* over an hour and a half ahead of the next Two-Tonner and were right in the middle of the 50-Footers. While approaching the rock we had decided that our strategy should be to sail low and fast on the way back to the Scillies since this would keep us in stronger wind all the way back. As it turned out, all the 50-Footers had decided to go straight down the rhumb line. We then had the really difficult tactical decision of whether to keep to our original strategy and split from the fleet or to take a tow (giving us a two-knot speed gain) and ignore our plan. In the event the latter choice won and we took a tow from one of the 50-Footers which was great - for a while. Eventually the wind died where we were and the rest of the Two-Tonners were able to come up behind us, see that we were stopped and sail low around us. If only we had ignored short-term tactics and stayed with our planned strategy!

10.9 THE GYBE MARK

General principles

As at most other marks, it is not the actual rounding of the mark which is important but your position after the rounding is complete. In this case the critical factor when rounding in the company of other yachts will nearly always be to get to windward after the rounding and not to allow yourself to be forced to round outside a raft of other yachts.

Rounding alone/ahead

If going into the buoy either alone or ahead of the pack, then the rounding should be relatively straightforward as long as your crew have practised the actual gybing manoeuvre often enough. Go in slightly wide, commence the gybe before the buoy if at all possible so that by the buoy itself you are ready to settle down onto the new course immediately. Then watch the yachts behind to ensure that you keep your wind clear without sailing too high on the next leg.

160 Mark rounding

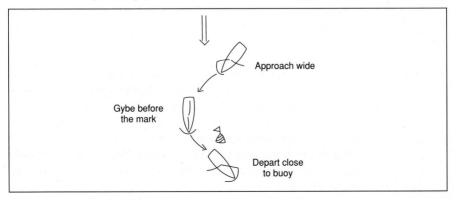

Approach wide

Gybe before
the mark

Depart close
to buoy

Getting an inside overlap

If you are in the less fortunate position of being behind another yacht (or yachts) then as you approach you will obviously try to get inside with an overlap. If achieved by two boat lengths from the buoy this will allow you to round as you please. Timing will be critical, you must establish the overlap in time for the other yacht(s) to be able to keep clear and they must recognize that the overlap has been established.

In any protest it will be up to the yacht coming from behind to prove that the overlap was established in good time and this can often be difficult. If in doubt, it can often be worth having your bowman run to the front of your boat when you think an overlap has been established to call positively to that effect. The rules actually say that hailing, while not proof in its own right will at least help in a disputed case. From the other point of view, the yacht ahead should have someone at the stern looking across and either accepting or denying the overlap - once again in a positive manner. One question which will normally be asked in a protest involving a dispute over when or if an overlap was established is: 'Where was the witness positioned on the yacht?' If you were back in the cockpit saying that you were able to judge that your bow was overlapped the yacht ahead by a metre or so, your case will be fairly weak.

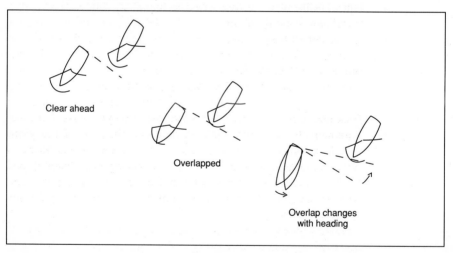

Clear ahead

Overlapped

Overlap changes
with heading

161 Overlap
situations

Once the yacht behind has established an overlap while outside two boat lengths from the buoy, if the overlap is broken thereafter it will then be up to the outside yacht to prove his case and to show that the overlap was actually broken while still more than two boat lengths from the mark.

One point to remember is that if you are trying to get and claim water at the gybe mark fairly late in the proceedings, this will inevitably put more pressure on your crew since they will not be able to set up for the gybe in a relaxed manner with plenty of time. Only try the tactic if you feel that your crew is good enough to cope with the situation.

No water

Whether you have been trying to get an inside overlap or are just a little bit further behind, there will come a time when the decision must be taken that an inside berth is not a possibility. The difficulty then will be that, since getting inside is not possible, the next priority must be to not be on the outside of other boats. It will be far better to go round just behind another yacht, on her transom and ready to pounce if she makes a mistake, rather than being on the outside, travelling further and ending up to leeward in dirty air after the mark rounding.

This is one of the times when it can often pay to slow down a little or sail wide for a moment or two in order to ensure that you can stay behind the yacht immediately ahead. If there are yachts outside him they can usually be ignored, since they will be unable to get at you even if you have no rights of water over them. In this way it should be possible to minimize the damage caused by being unable to get inside prior to the mark. A well-executed gybe should set you into a good position for the next leg, while breathing down the neck of the yacht ahead will sometimes force him to make errors.

One of the big dangers when approaching the gybe mark is coming in fast, hoping to find room inside, realizing at the last moment that this is impossible and being unable to slow down enough to stay behind. The only options here are bad ones. You could stay inside and leave the buoy on the wrong side, then come back and re-round - this would obviously lose you masses of time. Alternatively, you may opt to swing to windward of the yacht ahead and go around the outside. If there is only one yacht to worry about and there are no others following close behind, then the loss should not be too great, but if there is a pack to go around or other competitors are breathing down your neck, then the losses could be catastrophic.

During one of the inshore races of the 1987 Admiral's Cup, the British yacht *Juno* had just this situation at the gybe mark. She came from behind with good speed and claimed water on a whole gaggle of yachts. The inside one said 'no way' and shut her out leaving *Juno* with too much speed to stay behind and nowhere else to go except around the outside. She lost about eight places in this one mark rounding. Incidentally, she was unable to prove her claim at a subsequent protest hearing because, as always, it is very difficult to prove that you have established an overlap in time.

Inside is better than ahead

**10.10
THE LEEWARD
MARK**

Going around the leeward mark in close company with another yacht, the ideal position to be in is inside the other yacht, with rights for water. This means that not only will he have to sail further in his rounding but will also be to leeward after the mark and will not be able to prevent you from tacking immediately after the buoy, if that is your plan.

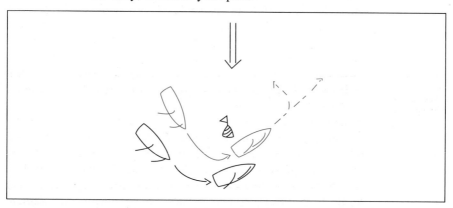

162 Inside at the mark is best

If the following yacht is actually clear astern, then he will probably exit from the mark still right on your stern and will have a certain amount of tactical advantage in the ensuing few seconds. The boat which is clear ahead has to abide by rule 41.2 and must have enough room to complete a tack before the following boat needs to start keeping clear or else she may not tack.

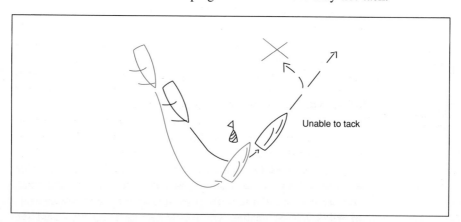

Unable to tack

163 If astern round well to get the advantage

Making sure that you force the following boat to go outside is often a subtle game of timing and slowing your boat down, once you are safely inside the two boat length circle. The tailing yacht will have little option but to swing wide and go around the outside, unless of course she anticipates your move and slows down herself to stay behind you.

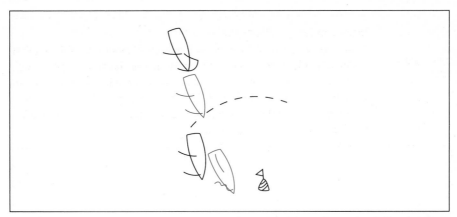

164 Slow down to force the boat astern outside

If the leading yacht has been unable to force the following boat to go outside and she is therefore exiting from the buoy immediately behind it will nearly always pay the leading yacht to luff sharply as soon as she is clear of the buoy. This will prevent the yacht behind from getting to windward and should help to make it possible for the yacht ahead to tack if that is necessary. Obviously the yacht behind should also luff just as sharply in order to keep the initiative.

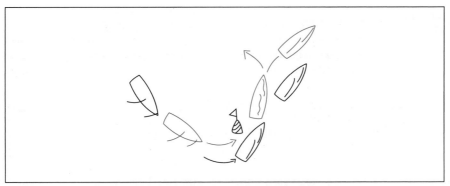

165 If ahead - luff hard to keep advantage

Port or starboard tack on the approach?

There are merits to suggest both port and starboard approaches to a normal port rounding at the leeward mark. While still more than two boat lengths from the buoy there is the obvious advantage to being on starboard tack that you will have the right of way. The other big advantage is that if you have judged your approach correctly and are coming into the buoy on the starboard layline, this will automatically put you on the inside of any yachts on the port layline.

The only real problem is one of crewing, if you come to the mark on starboard gybe and have to leave the buoy to port, you will of course have to gybe to go round the buoy. In light-to-moderate airs this should not present any real problems as long as your crew can perform a float drop, but on a windy day it will necessitate an early spinnaker drop and lots of hard work during the rounding. There will always be a danger that the inside yacht will lose out by virtue of the outside yacht having an easier spinnaker drop.

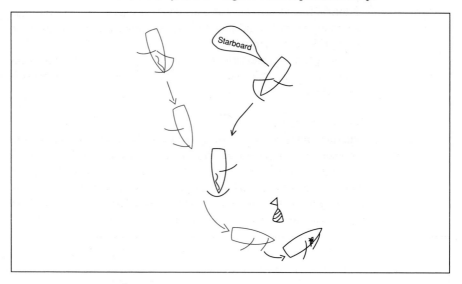

166 Simple drop often pays

Indecision

In close racing the tactical situation will be quite complex and may be changing all the time. This can make it difficult to decide what sort of drop is going to be called for and even which gybe your final, final approach will be on. In this sort of case there must come a time when simple crewing considerations outweigh tactics and the bowman needs to have a 'red light' time - after which you as tactician are not allowed to change your mind again.

I recall one race during a Sardinia Cup when I was navigating for Harold Cudmore on *Turkish Delight* when we came down the run in very close company with two other yachts. The situation got pretty tense as the leeward mark got nearer and since we were gybing on every shift in order to keep just ahead of another yacht, it was impossible to forecast the type of drop that was going to be required. The bowman did his best but Harold put in just one more gybe before the genoa went up and left no time for another change at the bow. We went round the mark ahead - but with the genoa still on the deck.

General points

10.11 RUNNING DOWNWIND

When in the lead it is much more difficult to be tactically safe while running downwind, than at any other time. This is because most of the initiative is with the yachts that are behind. They get all the wind shifts first, they decide whether to sit on the wind of the yacht ahead or not and so on. This does not mean that it is impossible to be tactically aware while leading the fleet, just that the options are limited.

It is vital to keep clear air when running and to sail to the target speeds and angles that suit your yacht whenever possible (see chapter 7). As tactician it is important to remember that the wind is coming from behind and so a lot of concentration needs to be put into looking behind.

The general principle that you should stay between your competitor(s) and the next mark applies equally well here as it does when going upwind.

Cover and clear air

The turbulence generated by a set of sails will be at its worst when the yacht is running square. At this time there will be little airflow over the sails and so they will act as a great big barrier to the wind. Even when a yacht is keeping the airflow over her sails by reaching up a little, there will still be a lot of turbulence downwind of her sails as shown in diagram 167.

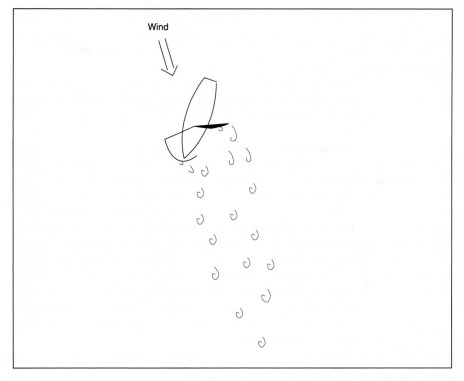

Wind

167 Dirty air on a run

Ultimately, the area of turbulent wind will be travelling directly downwind and not quite down the line of the windex because of the effect of boat speed on the apparent wind angle. However, when close to leeward of the sails, 'down windex' is a good approximation of the area of concern. If a yacht is sailing in turbulent air, the trimmers should be able to feel the difference as should a top-class helmsman: the whole boat and the wind will just feel not quite right.

Sometimes one sail will be clear of the effects of a yacht behind, while another sail will be affected. This is a point which needs to be considered at all times; your polars may not show a real decrease in performance but you can be sure that it will be there and the yacht in dirty air will be losing out all the time. It is obviously much easier to feel dirt on the spinnaker than on the mainsail, but both are important, so get used to looking behind and judging where the dirt is coming from.

Attacking from behind

If you are attacking a competitor from behind, the ultimate aim will often be to force her past the layline to allow yourself the opportunity to get inside with an overlap. To do this you need to use your wind shadow as a weapon, forcing gybes when the defending yacht is going the 'wrong way' by blanketing her and encouraging her to continue by deliberately staying just to the inside when she is going the way that the attacking yacht favours. Even a long way before the layline it is possible to use the same basic tactics to force and herd the yacht ahead as desired.

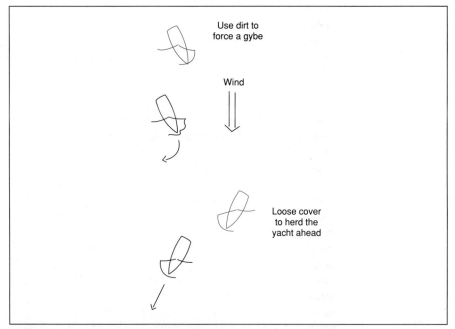

Use dirt to force a gybe

Wind

Loose cover to herd the yacht ahead

168 Use of loose or heavy cover downwind

Get the inside overlap

As the leeward mark is approached on the run, the important tactical consideration should be to get an inside overlap on any yachts close ahead. If rounding the mark to port this is made easier because the yacht outside will be unable to gybe and gain control because to do so would be to put her onto port tack with no rights.

It is often possible to force errors on the yacht ahead by keeping her under pressure, staying just about on her wind, to encourage her to luff out of dirt, and as soon as she does this gybing quickly inside her, thus gaining the overlap.

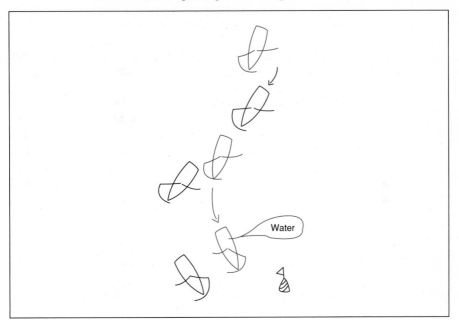

169 Use dirty air to force errors

Use the yacht behind to signal shifts

In general terms, if running as square as possible in a shifty wind, it is advantageous to gybe on wind shifts (see downwind strategy in chapter 9) and because the yacht behind will get any shift first the tendency will be for them to gybe before the yacht ahead. However, if the leading yacht of a pair is watching closely, the very fact that the following yacht has gybed will normally mean that a shift is on its way. If this is perceived to be the case, the yacht ahead can often make a gain by gybing just before the shift arrives so as to be on the correct gybe when it reaches her, a few seconds later. Waiting for the shift to arrive before starting to gybe will inevitably mean a delay (even with top-class crews it takes a few seconds to gybe) during which time potential advantage is being lost.

Defending downwind

In general terms if a yacht close behind is attacking it is very difficult to defend while running. If the attacker sits to windward with you in his wind shadow then it is normally best to luff slightly to keep in clear air. The problem then is that the attacker may respond and also sail higher, thus starting a reverse kind of luffing duel.

If this happens the only recourse is to gybe out of the situation, hoping to be able to complete your gybe before the following yacht can do so and then staying ahead of her wind shadow as in diagram 170. If she manages to gybe first each time, then it is likely that she will still be on your wind. Gybing often will prevent the yacht behind from settling down into a good attacking position and the ultimate winner will be the yacht which is better at gybing and which picks the most advantageous times to gybe.

170 Good gybing to break cover

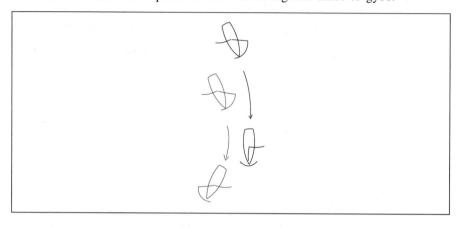

The attacker will be trying to force the defender outside the laylines or into a generally disadvantageous position and the best defence if this happens may well be to slow down suddenly, allow the attacker to put you in her wind shadow and then as soon as she is outside your line gybe to the inside, thus breaking the pattern of cover.

171 Another time to slow down!

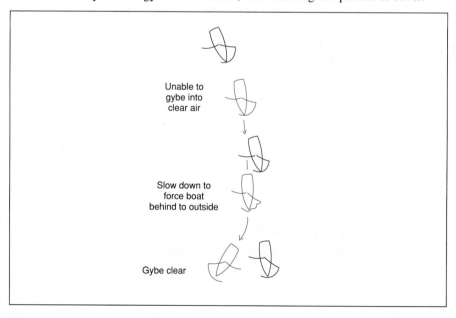

Unable to
gybe into
clear air

Slow down to
force boat
behind to outside

Gybe clear

Starboard tack?

The finish line is normally much shorter than the start line and so it gets congested. Added to this, the fact that one end is normally favoured (see chapter 9 - strategy) and this can add up to congestion even if only two or three yachts are finishing together.

Unless strategy up the beat dictates otherwise, it is always safer to plan to have your final approach on starboard tack since otherwise it is always possible to be forced to tack and maybe lose a place. This does not mean that you need to be on the layline very early, it is just the final few boat lengths which can be very critical. The message from this is that the port layline is potentially dangerous.

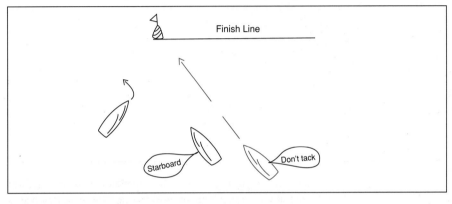

172 Port layline can be dangerous

Sailing an opponent past the layline

If just behind an opponent and on his weather hip, he will not be able to tack directly in front of you, especially if you are both on starboard tack. It is therefore possible (and perfectly legal) to continue until you are just past the layline, then tack and probably come out ahead.

If you are the yacht ahead, the defence against this happening is to ensure that you stay inside any close competitors to prevent them getting on your weather hip in the first place. If you have allowed someone to get into an attacking position, then this could be one of the times when some fairly extreme luffing would come in useful.

173 Sail your opponent past the line

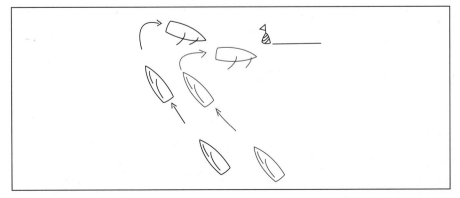

Shooting the line

As you reach the line, it will nearly always pay to shoot over the line at right angles to it, since with your momentum this will be the fastest way to finish. It is, however, very important before doing this that you are sure of the exact position of the line.

In one race at Dartmouth, we came to the finish at the committee-boat end of a line with a huge committee boat. The sailing instructions had not precisely defined the line and we shot head to wind around the stern of the boat. Some 10 seconds later we were still coasting head to wind when we eventually got a finishing signal - the man sighting the line was right at the bow of the committee boat! This did not lose us very much in time, but since it was a handicap race and we were beaten into second place by one second on corrected time it certainly lost us that place.